The Science of

Food and Cooking

Third Edition

Allan G. Cameron

Illustrated by
Ron Hayward Associates Limited

Hodder & Stoughton

LONDON SYDNEY AUCKLAND TORONTO

To Heather, Ruth and Anne

British Library Cataloguing in Publication Data

Cameron, Allan Gillies
    The science of food and cooking, 3rd ed.
    1. Food
    I. Title
    641.3   TX354

    ISBN 0 7131 0945 9

First published 1973
Third edition 1985
Reprinted 1989

Printed in Great Britain for the educational
publishing division of Hodder and Stoughton Ltd,
Mill Road, Dunton Green, Sevenoaks, Kent by
Page Bros (Norwich) Ltd, Norwich, Norfolk

Preface

The aim of this new edition, as of the previous ones, is to give not just the facts about food and cooking but an *understanding* of them. It seeks to answer simply the 'how' and 'why' questions about food, including its nature and how it is stored, processed, preserved, cooked, eaten and digested. It has been written for pupils in secondary schools, who will appreciate the straightforward style and many photographs, tables and diagrams as well as the activity sections, questions and keypoints. It is intended to appeal to both girls and boys and should be useful for CSE and GCE 'O' level exams.

This new edition retains a strong emphasis on cooking, particularly the effects of cooking on nutrients, flavour, colour and texture. It includes a new final chapter on diet, health and disease reflecting the remarkable interest shown in this important topic not only by nutritionists and doctors but also by the public and the media. Up-dating and rewriting has occurred throughout the text to take into account the many changes and advances of the last few years.

A.G.C.

Acknowledgements

The Publishers would like to thank the following for their permission to reproduce copirght photographs.

J. Allan Cash: pp. 28, 107 & 117 t & b; Australian News & Information Bureau: p. 110; Bakery Information Service: p. 214; B.B.C. Hulton Picture Library: p. 10; Birds Eye Ltd. p. 165; British Egg Information Service: p. 206; British Red Cross Society: p. 143; Boots Co. Ltd. p. 100; Bush Boake Allen Ltd. pp. 232 & 235; Camera Press: p. 12 l & r; Central Press: p. 4 (all); Conway Picture Library: pp. 67, 83, 85, 120, 122, 145, 147 t & b, 177, 204 (all), 212 (all), 236 & 238; CSIRO: p. 155t; Domestos Ltd. p. 186; The Electricity Council: p. 127; The Flour Advisory Bureau: pp. 59 & 208 (all); W. J. Garnett: p. 36; Guy's Hospital: p. 118; 'Here's Health' Magazine: p. 242; Sarah Hobson: p. 111; Nina-Anne Kaye: p. 133; The Kenya Coffee Industry: p. 121; Diana Lanham: p. 51; Long Ashton Research Station: p. 162; The Lord Rank Research Centre: p. 197; J. Lyons & Co. Ltd. p. 62 (all); Dr. Mercer: p. 36; Odhams Press Ltd. pp. 135 & 220; Phoebus Picture Library: p. 20 (all); Rank, Hovis McDougall Ltd. p. 159 l & r; St. Bartholomew's Hospital: p. 113; Catherine Shakespeare Lane: p. 180; Smedleys Ltd. p. 161; Studio Lisa Ltd. p. 140; Tate & Lyle Ltd: p. 68 t & b; Tesco Stores Ltd: pp. 152 & 163; Tower Housewares ltd. p. 196; UNICEF photograph by Jack Ling: p. 126; Unigate Ltd. pp. 53 (all) & 84 (all); Unilever Educational Publications: pp. 52 l & r, 153 & 155 c & b; United Nations: p. 95t; Worthington Foods inc. p. 95b.

Contents

1 The Need for Food— and its Nature

THE BODY AS A LIVING MACHINE

In this book we shall be talking about food and about how it affects us. In order to see the nature of the link between food and ourselves, let us first of all think about what we mean by *life*. Life is very difficult to explain, but it is usually easy to recognize. Living things—whether animal or vegetable—have certain features in common. For instance, a young boy and a young apple tree are similar to each other in some ways. The most obvious likeness between them is that they are both growing. Also, they both need food and water and air if they are to keep on living, and this is true even when they have finished growing. Another very important feature about fully-grown living things is that they can reproduce themselves. The apples on an apple tree, for example, contain seeds from which new trees may develop. Similarly, a man produces sex cells which, when united with female sex cells, lead to the formation of new life. Human beings are like all other living things in that unless they are provided with a regular supply of food, water and air they die.

In some ways we can think of ourselves as living machines. A car engine works by using petrol as a fuel, and when the petrol and air are mixed and ignited inside the cylinder an explosion takes place that pushes the piston downwards and causes the car to move. In our case we use energy foods as fuel, and after being taken into our bodies such food enables us to move and keep warm. Unlike the reaction in a car engine this is a slow steady process that goes on all the time without our noticing it. Both the car engine and the human body are kept warm by the action of fuel inside them.

1

The nature of the body

Before we can understand *why* we need food, we must take a closer look at our bodies. A solid framework of bone protects our more delicate parts and gives strength to the whole body structure. We call this framework the skeleton, and though it is strong it is also flexible so that we may move the various parts of our bodies easily. The skeleton acts as a shield for the system of organs inside us. At the hub of this system is the heart, which works an amazing transport system that reaches into every corner of our bodies, from the tops of our heads to the tips of our toes. The heart is a pump that makes blood flow round the body, and the blood takes food and oxygen to every part of the body and in exchange removes waste material. The main organs of the body are made from tissue material such as muscle tissue and nerve tissue. These tissues have their special jobs to do; muscle tissue for instance, is concerned with all body movement.

The body is a very complex machine with many different organs, each of which has its own task to perform. The lungs are concerned with supplying oxygen to the bloodstream and removing the waste gas carbon dioxide. Kidneys are concerned with removing liquid waste matter as urine. The brain is the main organ of the nervous system, being the principal controller of our actions and thinking. Each of these organs can only work if it is supplied with food, and this applies to all the other organs and tissues of the body which we have not mentioned. Think now of what we need from food to keep all these organs and tissues working properly.

★ ? What features do all living things have in common?

Why do we need food?

1. Food for energy. It is well known that 'You can't get something for nothing', and this idea may be applied to the use of energy by our bodies. Every time we move we use up energy; as we cannot get energy for nothing, it follows that we must replace it by some means or other. One of the functions of food is to replenish our store of energy.

When we move quickly we use up energy quickly; when we move slowly we use up energy more slowly. Even when we appear to be resting—as when we are asleep—we are using up energy

2

simply because we are living. This is because the inside of the body is never at rest. Even when we *appear* to be resting the heart must keep on beating and the lungs must keep on working, to mention only two organs. Both these processes involve movement and movement uses up energy. So simply to keep alive requires an additional supply. One of the things that food must do, therefore, is to supply us with energy.

2. Food for body-building. We have seen that growth, amongst other things, distinguishes living things from non-living. While we are young our bodies are developing; so during this time growth is very obvious. But even when we stop growing outwardly, our bodies continue to make new material. For instance, our hair and our nails keep on growing and when we cut or burn ourselves new skin is formed to replace the old. Indeed, skin and all our other tissues are continually being renewed. Remembering that we cannot get something for nothing, we realize that the material needed for growth and the renewal of our tissues must come from somewhere; as you will have guessed, it comes from food. Food then is needed for body-building—to enable us to grow, to repair and renew tissues and to create new life; that is to reproduce ourselves.

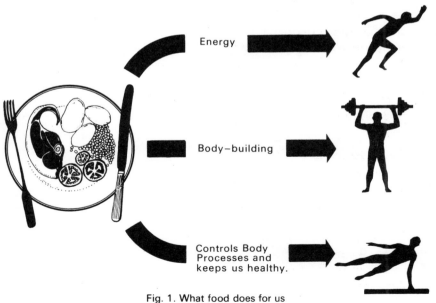

Energy

Body–building

Controls Body Processes and keeps us healthy.

Fig. 1. What food does for us

Food is needed (1) for energy, (2) for body-building and (3) for control

3. Food for control of body processes. Many processes are going on inside our bodies all the time and it is fairly obvious that if confusion is to be avoided, each process must be regulated so that it does not interfere with any other. The situation is rather like that at a busy road junction. If the traffic is to be kept moving without any collisions taking place, some form of control—a policeman or traffic lights—is needed. Inside our bodies it is food that is used to control our body processes and keep us healthy.

★★★ **Keypoint.** Food is also needed to provide bulk or volume. The body would not be healthy if our food consisted of nothing but tablets; we need the chewy foods that provide us with bulk or *dietary fibre*.

What are nutrients?

We cannot live by eating anything that we choose. For example, it is impossible to live by eating nothing but cream cakes. We must choose what we eat—that is our *diet*—with care, so that it keeps us healthy. It will only do this if it carries out the three jobs mentioned above. And it can only do this if it contains substances called *nutrients*. Although there are hundreds of different foods there are only a few types of nutrients.

★★★ **Keypoint.** There are five types of nutrient and these are: *carbohydrates, fats, proteins, mineral elements* and *vitamins*.

Food provides the body with nutrients and also with bulk. Some foods are *pure* or *refined* meaning that they contain little or nothing that is not a nutrient. White sugar, for example, is said to be pure for it contains nothing but carbohydrate. At the other extreme, we eat substances that contain no nutrients at all. Bran (see page 55), for example, contains hardly any nutrients and is nearly all dietary fibre.

Salt is another example of a food that is pure; it contains nothing but the mineral elements *sodium* and *chlorine*. Pepper however does not contain any nutrients, neither does it contain any dietary fibre—it is not really a food at all because it does not provide the body with anything that it needs. It merely adds flavour to other foods.

5

In contrast to those foods, such as sugar and salt, which contain one type of nutrient there are others which contain several. Most foods are of this kind and some very valuable foods, such as milk, contain a variety of nutrients and can carry out all three of the jobs that food must do.

★★★ **Keypoint.** Many valuable foods provide us with both a variety of nutrients as well as dietary fibre, e.g. bread.

Much of what follows will be concerned either with the nutrients which are found in various foods or with the effect that these nutrients have on our bodies. The study of these effects is called *nutrition*. For example, if our diet is well chosen we shall not only get a supply of all six nutrients, but we shall get them in the right proportions for our bodies' needs. In such cases our bodies receive all that they need to remain healthy and we enjoy good nutrition. On the other hand, if our diet gives us too little of the nutrients we need our health suffers and we are said to be in a state of *under-nutrition*. If our diet continues to give us a smaller and smaller supply of nutrients we eventually starve (see page 10).

Each nutrient carries out at least one of the three tasks of food, and some nutrients are able to do more than one job. Whereas fat, for example, only supplies us with energy, other nutrients, such as mineral elements and vitamins, both control body processes and are concerned with growth and repair. The jobs that the various nutrients do is shown in Fig. 2. Important foods which provide these nutrients are also shown.

★★★ **Keypoint.** Starchy foods, such as bread, are good sources of carbohydrate. Body-building proteins are found particularly in such foods as meat, fish, eggs and cheese, while butter, margarine and lard are important sources of fat.

Using Fig. 2 as your guide you will now be able to try the following questions, working out which foods are related to which nutrients.

★ **?** Starchy foods such as bread and potatoes are good sources of which nutrient?

★ **?** Meat, fish, eggs and cheese are useful body-building foods because they are good sources of which nutrient?

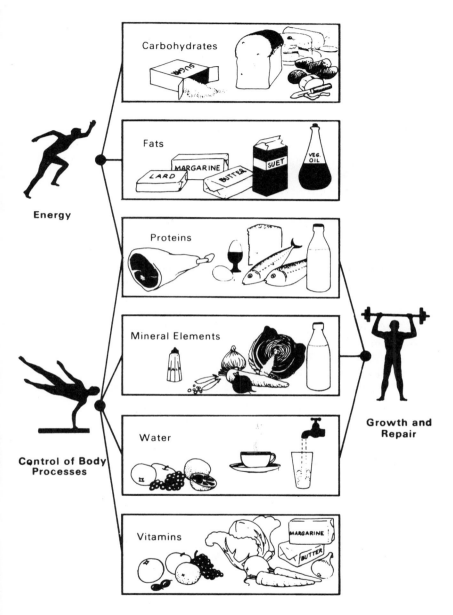

Fig. 2. The nutrients and water—showing *some* important foods in which they are found and also their tasks in the body

★ ? Butter and margarine are rich sources of which two nutrients?
★ ? Sugar contains one nutrient only. What is it? Milk contains several, name two.

What is food made of?

When we pick up a piece of coal we may wonder what it contains. Coal is mainly *carbon*, and carbon is an example of an *element*, which means that it is a simple kind of material which cannot be split up into anything simpler. If we start hammering a piece of coal, we shall split it up into smaller and smaller pieces until we have ground it into a fine dust. But it will still be mainly carbon. Let us now imagine that a speck of carbon was broken down into even smaller pieces. Soon the speck would become invisible and eventually it would become so small that it would be impossible to split it any further. We would then have the smallest piece of carbon that could exist. Such a particle is called an *atom*.

Every element is made up of atoms which means that everything we know—whether solid, liquid or gas—is atomic. All the atoms of an element are alike, but they differ in size from the atoms of every other element. It is very difficult to imagine the size of atoms because they are so very small. An illustration may perhaps make this clearer. The smallest atoms are those of the gas *hydrogen*. If we were to take a hollow pin's head and fill it with hydrogen, we should have enough hydrogen atoms to give several *million* to each person living on the earth.

Although we know of about one hundred elements, only a dozen or so of these are important in foods. These elements are listed opposite with a brief description of what they are like. The elements which are most often found in foods are at the top of the table.

Hydrogen atom

Hydrogen molecule

Fig. 3

ELEMENTS OF IMPORTANCE IN FOODS

Name of element	Description of element
Carbon	Black solid
Hydrogen	Lightest gas known
Oxygen	Colourless gas
Nitrogen	Colourless gas
Sulphur	Yellow solid
Sodium	Soft silvery metal
Calcium	Silvery metal
Potassium	Soft silvery metal
Chlorine	Yellow poisonous gas
Phosphorus	Red solid
Iron	Greyish metal
Iodine	Violet solid
Fluorine	Yellowish gas

Atoms rarely exist on their own. They normally link up in groups of two or more, and such a group is called a *molecule*. Thus hydrogen gas is made up of molecules of hydrogen, and each molecule consists of two atoms (Fig. 3).

When atoms of different elements join together they form a *compound*. For example, water is a simple compound and one water molecule consists of two atoms of hydrogen linked to one atom of oxygen (Fig. 4).

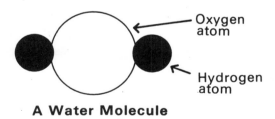

A Water Molecule

Fig. 4

It may seem surprising that some of the elements found in food are poisonous gases or metallic solids. The explanation of this is that these elements never occur free in foods, but are in the form of compounds—and compounds have quite different properties from the elements of which they are made. Thus water is a colourless liquid, though it is made up of two elements which are both

A well chosen diet gives good nutrition and helps us to remain healthy while a poor diet produces under-nutrition and health suffers

gases. When an atom of the metal sodium becomes joined to an atom of the poisonous gas chlorine a molecule of sodium chloride or salt is formed. As we have already noted, this is a food and has no similarity to the elements from which it is made.

Although only a few elements commonly occur in food, they can join together in a very large number of ways, so that many different compounds are found in foods. For example, all carbohydrates, all oils and fats and some vitamins are made up of the three elements carbon, hydrogen and oxygen. If we add two more elements—nitrogen and sulphur—we can also include most proteins. Considering proteins alone we find, probably to our surprise, that thousands of different proteins are found in foods.

ELEMENTS AND THE NUTRIENTS THEY FORM

Elements	Nutrients formed
Hydrogen and oxygen	Water
Hydrogen, oxygen and carbon	Fats, carbohydrates, some vitamins
Hydrogen, oxygen, carbon and nitrogen	Many proteins
Sodium and chlorine	Sodium chloride

The simplest molecules that occur in food—such as water and sodium chloride—are made up of only two or three atoms, and these molecules are very small indeed. Their smallness can be imagined more easily if we use an illustration.

★★★ **Keypoint.** If we could take one drop of water and magnify it until it was the size of the earth, a water molecule would only be about the size of a small apple (see photo on page 12).

Most of the compounds found in food are more complicated than water and salt. The simplest type of carbohydrate, such as glucose, contains 24 atoms in its molecule—6 atoms of carbon, 6 of oxygen and 12 of hydrogen. Fats are rather larger and a typical fat molecule contains about 170 atoms. Some molecules found in food contain a very large number of atoms indeed. Proteins, for example, are very complex and a large protein molecule will contain several hundred thousand atoms as you can see

11

A raindrop magnified until it appears to be the same size as the earth as seen from an Apollo spacecraft

by looking at the photograph on page 23. However, even such large molecules are very small indeed by normal standards, and are far too small to be seen by even the best microscope.

★★ **Activity.** List all the main foods you had to eat yesterday. With the help of Fig. 2, list alongside each food the nutrients it contained. Do you think you might have gone short of any nutrient?

★★★ **Keypoint.** All food is chemical in nature and is composed of molecules of various elements. Even a delicious steak is nothing more than a collection of chemical substances.

2 The Nature of Nutrients

What exactly are nutrients like? That is the question we are going to answer now.

★ **?** Before we discuss the nutrients can you remember what they are called?

WATER

We have already discussed the structure of water and seen how each molecule is made up of two atoms of hydrogen and one atom of oxygen. We do not need to say any more about water except that though we do not usually refer to water as a nutrient, it is nevertheless essential. Water is a part of nearly all foods and many foods, such as fruit and leafy vegetables, are nearly all water. Even so-called 'dry' foods, such as bread, are about one-third water.

★ **?** What foods can you think of that contain practically no water?

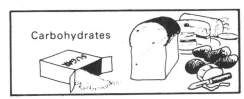

CARBOHYDRATES

★★ **Activity.** List the main items you had for lunch yesterday. Decide the main nutrient in each item. Which nutrient formed the bulk of your meal?

13

You have probably just found out that the nutrient we eat most of in a typical meal is *carbohydrate*. Most of the bulky foods in our diet—such as potatoes, bread, cakes and biscuits—are mainly carbohydrate.

We are like other animals in that we cannot make carbohydrates for ourselves. Luckily for us, plants have the power to build up or *synthesize* carbohydrates. Therefore, in order to get the carbohydrates that our bodies need, we can use plants—or animals that have fed on plants—as food.

Plants build carbohydrates from very simple starting materials. In fact all they need is the gas carbon dioxide, water and sunlight. As carbohydrates are energy-providing substances they must contain a store of energy. This stored energy is obtained from sunlight when carbohydrate is made out of carbon dioxide and water. This process is called *photosynthesis*, which means 'put together by light', and it occurs in the green leaves of the plant in the presence of daylight.

At first photosynthesis leads to the formation of simple sugars, such as *glucose*. Carbon dioxide contains carbon and oxygen linked together. Therefore, when carbon dioxide combines with water, a substance containing carbon, hydrogen and oxygen is formed. All carbohydrates are made up of these three elements, and in the simple case of glucose each molecule is small. In later stages of photosynthesis larger carbohydrate molecules are built up. The end product of this process is *starch*, which is the form in which plants store energy for future use.

★ ? What 3 elements are used as building bricks in the formation of carbohydrates?

★★★ **Keypoint.** In photosynthesis:

plant + sunlight
+ carbon dioxide ⎫⟶ glucose ⟶ starch
+ water ⎭

Simple sugars

Glucose is an example of a *simple sugar* or *monosaccharide*. It is found in grapes and other sweet fruits and also in honey. Other examples are *fructose*, which occurs with glucose in sweet fruits and honey, and *galactose*, which is not found in food. Both fructose and

14

galactose contain the same number of carbon, hydrogen and oxygen atoms as glucose. The only difference between them is the way in which the atoms are arranged in the molecule. Molecules of glucose, fructose and galactose are shown in Fig. 5. They have all been given the same shape to indicate that they are similar, but they have been shaded differently to indicate that they are not exactly the same. It will be understood that here, and elsewhere in the book, the shapes given to molecules are not their actual shapes; the shapes in the diagrams are chosen merely to help you to understand the way molecules are built up or changed in reactions.

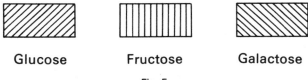

Glucose   Fructose   Galactose

Fig. 5

Glucose, fructose and galactose all have similar properties. They are all white, crystalline solids and they are all sweet. They dissolve easily in water to form colourless, sweet solutions.

★ ? Packets of glucose and fructose can be bought in shops to be used in place of sugar. Where do these sugars occur in food?

Double sugars

Double sugars or *disaccharides* are built up from two simple sugar molecules. The most familiar double sugar is ordinary household

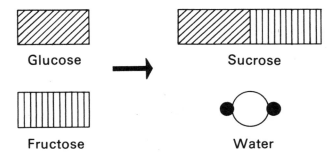

Fig. 6. The formation of sucrose and water from glucose and fructose

15

sugar or *sucrose*. Sucrose is built up from one molecule of glucose and one molecule of fructose and that, of course, is why it is called a *double* sugar (Fig. 6).

There are two other important double sugars. One is *lactose* or *milk sugar*, which is built up from one molecule of glucose and one of galactose. As its name suggests, milk sugar is found in the milk of animals. The other important double sugar is *maltose* or *malt sugar*, which is built up from two molecules of glucose.

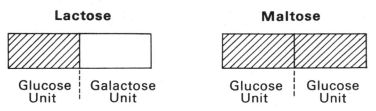

Fig. 7. The structure of lactose and maltose, showing how they are built up from two simple sugar units

Double sugars are white, sweet crystalline solids and they dissolve in water to give clear, colourless solutions.

Sucrose is by far the most important sugar in our diet; in Great Britain we consume roughly a kilogramme per person per week. It has a very important property which we shall now consider. If we warm a solution of sucrose in water, to which a little acid has been added, we find that the sucrose is broken down into the simple sugars glucose and fructose from which it was built. This splitting of the sucrose molecule is brought about by the water, though the acid which is present helps to speed up the reaction. Such a splitting by water is called a *hydrolysis*. You can picture it as shown in Fig. 8.

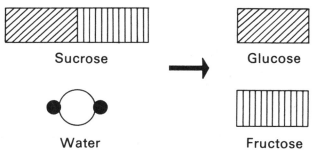

Fig. 8. The hydrolysis of sucrose into glucose and fructose

16

If you look carefully at this reaction you will notice that it is the reverse of what happened when a sucrose molecule was built up from glucose and fructose as shown in Fig. 6. This suggests that the build-up of sucrose is not simply the linking together of glucose and fructose. It is a reaction which involves the splitting out of one molecule of water. We shall see in what follows that water has a most important role to play in very many of the processes concerned both in the build-up of foods in plants and in their later break-down in man and animals.

The mixture of glucose and fructose formed by hydrolysing sugar is called *invert-sugar*. Honey—which is made by bees—is mainly invert-sugar together with about one-fifth water and small amounts of flavouring. Bees collect nectar—which is mainly sucrose—from flowers, and as the sucrose passes through the bee it is converted by hydrolysis into invert-sugar. The special flavour of honey depends upon the flavourings in the flowers from which the bees collect their nectar. For instance, if you have ever tasted heather honey and clover honey you will have noticed that each has a distinctive flavour of its own. This is due to the different flavouring substances found in heather and clover flowers. Long ago, before man had discovered the secret of how to get sugar from sugar beet or sugar cane, honey was an important part of the diet, being the only sweetening agent known.

SUMMARY TABLE OF SUGARS

Sugar	Sweetness	Food in which it occurs
Sucrose	4	Jams, honey, cakes, biscuits
Glucose	3	Jams, honey, grapes
Fructose	5	Jams, honey, many fruits
Lactose	1	Milk, condensed milk
Maltose	2	Malt

When sucrose is hydrolysed into invert-sugar the process is known as *inversion*, and it is often an important process in food-making. Thus in making jam, fruit is boiled with added sugar, and in the presence of acids contained in the fruit, inversion occurs (see page 20). This is of great importance because invert-sugar prevents jam from crystallizing when it is stored. Invert-sugar must also be present in boiled sweets and toffee to prevent the crystallization that would otherwise occur. Crystallization is undesirable because it makes sweets gritty and 'sugary'.

★ ? Fruit drinks, made from fresh fruit and sucrose, also contain invert-sugar. Why is this?

★★ **Activity.** In the table on p. 17 you will see that the sweetness of sugars is given as a score. Collect as many of the sugars given in the table as possible, together with honey and syrup. Taste each in turn and put them in order of sweetness with the sweetest at the top and the least sweet at the bottom. How do your results compare with those in the table where the highest score is given to the sweetest sugar?

Polysaccharides

The main examples of polysaccharides (meaning *many sugars*) found in food are *starch* and *cellulose*. Like the simple sugars, polysaccharides are built up from simple materials in plants by photosynthesis. Although polysaccharide molecules are very much bigger than those of simple sugars, it is fairly easy to understand their construction because they are built from monosaccharide units, just like disaccharides.

Starch. Starch is made up of glucose units, which are linked together as indicated in Fig. 9. The diagram shows only a very small part of a starch molecule because a complete molecule contains many thousands of linked glucose units, which could not possibly all be shown in a single diagram. The starch molecule is rather like a long string of similar beads which are strung end to end.

Glucose
unit

Fig. 9. A small part of a starch molecule, showing four glucose units

Starch is stored by plants as a reserve supply of energy. It is found stored in the stems of plants as in the sago palm, in the tubers as in potatoes and in the roots as in cassava, from which tapioca is made. It is also found in seeds, such as the cereal grains —wheat, barley and oats—and in unripe fruit.

As more and more glucose units are joined together—each linkage involving the splitting out of one water molecule—the sugar-like properties are lost. Thus starch, which is a white solid, differs from the sugars in that it is not sweet and that it will not dissolve in cold water.

Fibre. Dietary fibre consists of that part of plant foods which cannot be digested by the body. Fibre is a complex mixture of substances but its four main constituents are the polysaccharides *pectin, cellulose* and *hemicellulose* and the non-polysaccharide *lignin,* which forms the hard, woody parts of plants. The fibre of different foods is very different; that of celery is stringy, fibrous and crunchy, that of bananas is smooth and soft while that of cereal grains is hard and chewy.

Pectin. The polysaccharide *pectin* has no direct value as a food, but is valuable as a setting agent in jam-making. Certain fruit, such as apples, plums and citrus fruit are rich in pectin, and so jam made from such fruit sets easily. The pectin is extracted by simmering the fruit (in water for such fruit as plums and damsons) for a period before sugar is added. Fruit containing little pectin—such as strawberries and marrow—are difficult to make into jam, and additional pectin or pectin-rich fruit may be added to promote setting.

Cellulose. Cellulose—like starch—is built up from large numbers of glucose units which become linked together through the splitting out of water molecules. The properties of cellulose are quite different from those of starch, however, because the linking process takes place in a slightly different way. Cellulose is found in fruits and vegetables, where it strengthens the walls of the plant; also in the husks of wheat and other cereal grains. Indeed, all forms of plant life—from the toughest tree-trunk to the softest cotton wool—contain cellulose.

Cellulose, like starch, has lost the sugar-like properties of glucose. It forms hair-like fibres which are not sweet and will not dissolve in water. You might expect that it would be possible to break down or hydrolyse cellulose into glucose molecules, just as it was possible to hydrolyse sucrose into the units from which it

Pectin is the main setting agent in jam; acid is also required for a good set. Fruit which are low in pectin and acid, such as strawberries, may be made into jam if acid (e.g. in the form of lemon juice) is added (1). Raspberry jam can be made from raspberries and sugar alone (2). After sugar has been added the fruit is boiled rapidly and poured into warm jars using a funnel (3). The jars are covered and sealed as soon as the jam is cold (4)

20

was built. Although it is possible to do this, it is much more difficult to carry out than was the case with sucrose and, as we shall see in the next chapter, this has an important consequence in digestion.

★ ? What is inversion; why is it important?

★ ? What are the main polysaccharides that occur in food?

★★★ **Keypoint.** Carbohydrates are the main sources of energy in our diet.

PROTEINS

We have seen that because animals cannot make their own carbohydrate they must obtain it from their food. In a similar way animals, including man, cannot make their own protein and so they have to obtain their protein needs from plants, which can make their own protein out of simple starting materials. Alternatively they can obtain their protein by eating animals which have themselves fed on plants.

In addition to the elements carbon, hydrogen and oxygen that are present in carbohydrates, proteins always contain nitrogen, often sulphur and sometimes phosphorus. Proteins are very complicated substances, but we can easily get some idea of their structure because they are built up from large numbers of fairly simple units called *amino acids*. A single protein molecule of average size will contain as many as 500 amino acid units.

Figure 10(a) shows the way in which amino acids link together to form a long-chain protein molecule. Every time that two amino acids join up a molecule of water is split out. This will remind you of what happened when glucose and fructose joined together to form sucrose, and it is indeed a similar sort of reaction. Do not think, however, that you know all about the structure of proteins because you know that they are made of long chains of linked amino acids. The chains of amino acids are not in simple straight lines, but are zig-zag shaped, coiled and linked to other chains in a variety of ways.

21

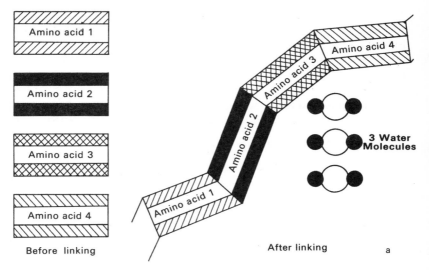

Fig. 10(a). A small portion of a protein molecule, showing the way it is built up from amino acids

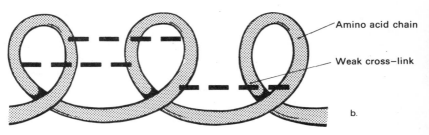

Fig. 10(b). The long chains of amino acids are coiled and the coils are held in position by weak cross-links that are easily broken

It is helpful to picture a protein as shown in Fig. 10(b). The chains are like coils with the loops of the coil held in position by weak cross-links. In most proteins found in food and in the body these coils are folded over each other to form a bulky shape. If you look closely at the photo on page 23 you can see the snake-like chain that gives shape to the molecule. You may be thinking that this is all rather complicated; well, it is! But if you can keep these pictures in your mind you will find it helpful in understanding what happens to protein foods when they are cooked.

22

The problem of trying to work out exactly what proteins are like is a very difficult one and scientists in different parts of the world have been trying to solve it for many years. Recently there has been exciting progress in this field, and we now know the complete structure of several proteins such as the one shown below.

This model will give you some idea of the complexity of proteins and you can see the way in which the many thousands of atoms are linked together.

If you compare Fig. 10 with Fig. 9, which shows part of a starch molecule, you will notice an important difference. Whereas a starch molecule contains the *same* unit repeated over and over again, a protein molecule contains a number of *different* units.

About 20 different amino acids are found in protein foods. This may not seem a very large number, but it means that there are a great many different ways in which they may be arranged. This can be appreciated if you remember that a protein molecule may contain 500 linked amino acids. With 20 *different* amino acids to choose from, almost endless arrangements are possible. In fact the number is so very large—more than a million, million, million— that it cannot be imagined!

Not all the 20 amino acids found in food proteins are present in any one protein, and this cuts down the number of possible arrangements. Even so you will see why thousands of different food proteins exist. Luckily for us we need not remember the names of all these different proteins, because the important thing about a protein is the amino acids that it contains.

Only the simplest proteins consist entirely of amino acids. Other proteins, called *conjugated* proteins, contain other types of unit in their molecule. For example, the protein *casein*, which is the main protein found in milk and cheese, contains a phosphorus compound linked to the amino acid units.

★★ **Activity.** Heat a little egg white gently. It is convenient to put the egg white into a test tube or other small container and heat this in a pan of water. Stir the egg white with a thermometer and note the temperature when the appearance of the egg white changes. How does the egg white change? Heat the water strongly until it boils; keep it boiling and note the change in the egg white.

★ ? What is the lowest temperature at which you can 'cook' an egg? Can you poach an egg if the water is not boiling?

How can we explain what happens to egg white when it is heated? Egg white is simply a watery solution of the protein *ovalbumin*. When this is heated the weak links that fix the protein in a particular shape (Fig. 10(b)) break and the coiled chains unfold. This is what was happening to the egg white when it became solid. The change is known as *coagulation*.

All proteins are very delicate substances and many are affected by heat in a similar way to egg white. Many are also affected by acids and alkalis and also by beating them. For instance, if you beat up egg white it becomes foamy and if you beat it long enough, the foam becomes quite stiff. This is because the ovalbumin has been partly coagulated. If the foam is heated, further coagulation occurs, and the foam becomes rigid. This is what happens in the making of meringues (see page 203).

★★★ **Keypoint.** Most food proteins are very delicate substances that coagulate, i.e. turn solid very easily. This change is important in protein cooking. Once proteins have coagulated they can't be changed back.—You can't unscramble scrambled egg!

★ ? What 4 elements are always found in proteins? Can you name 2 others that are often present?

★ ? Proteins are all built up from one type of unit; what is its name?

OILS AND FATS

Fats, such as butter and margarine, are familiar to us all. We recognize them at once by their appearance and smell, their greasy feel and taste and because they do not mix (or dissolve) with water. We say that they are insoluble in water.

★★ **Activity.** Take a selection of oils and fats. Put a drop of each oil (e.g. olive oil, cooking oil) on (a) filter paper and (b) grease-proof paper. Note the appearance of the paper when held up to a strong light. Repeat with the fats (e.g. lard, margarine, butter) by rubbing a little on to the paper.

★ ? Why are fatty foods not wrapped or packed in ordinary paper? Why are fatty marks on clothes difficult to remove?

24

Fats are similar to carbohydrates in two ways. First they contain the same three elements—carbon, hydrogen and oxygen —and second, they have the same role in the body—they provide us with energy. Fats are formed by the linking together of *glycerol* (or *glycerine*) with *fatty acids* as pictured in Fig. 11. You will notice that one molecule of fat is formed when one molecule of glycerol links with three molecules of fatty acid.

Fatty acids. You will be familiar with food acids such as acetic acid (vinegar) and citric acid (in lemon juice) and you can recognise that they are acids because of their sour taste. Acids which form fats are called *fatty acids.* For example, *butyric acid* forms butter fat while *palmitic acid* and *stearic acid* are found in most fats. All these fatty acids are known as *saturated* fatty acids but others are called *unsaturated.* They differ from saturated acids in that they contain less hydrogen. For example, *oleic acid* is a common unsaturated fatty acid and if hydrogen is added to it, it becomes the saturated fatty acid stearic acid.

Oleic acid + hydrogen → stearic acid

★★ **Activity.** Taste a little vinegar and then lemon juice. How would you describe their taste? Add a little blue litmus solution (or paper) to each. Note how the colour changes; this shows they are acids.

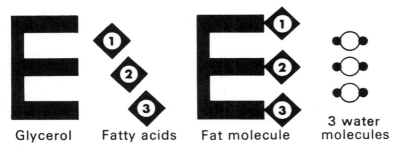

Glycerol   Fatty acids   Fat molecule   3 water molecules

Fig. 11. This shows how a fat molecule is built up from glycerol and fatty acids

25

Essential fatty acids. Fatty acids which contain much less hydrogen than the corresponding saturated acid are said to be *polyunsaturated*. *Linoleic acid* is an example of a polyunsaturated fatty acid (or PUFA for short) but it is also known as an *essential* fatty acid because it is essential to the healthy action of our body and must be provided by our food.

Saturated fats. When saturated fatty acids link with glycerol they form fats which are said to be *saturated*. Saturated fats are easy to recognise because they are hard rather than soft. Animal fats—such as butter, lard, suet and hard margarine—are typical examples of saturated fats. The fat in dairy products such as milk, cream and cheese is also mainly of the saturated variety.

Polyunsaturated oils and fats. When polyunsaturated fatty acids (PUFA) link with glycerol they form polyunsaturated oils or fats which are soft. (The main difference between an oil and a fat is that at normal room temperature an oil is liquid while a fat is solid.) Many vegetable oils such as corn oil, sunflower seed oil and soya bean oil are formed from PUFA as are the oils of most nuts and soft margarines made from oils rich in PUFA.

★★★ **Keypoint.** All the different types of fats and fatty acids mentioned above seem rather confusing but the difference is important because many people believe that too much saturated fat in our diet is unhealthy and that we should eat more polyunsaturated fats which may be healthier (see Chapter 13).

★★ **Activity.** Olive oil is one of the purest vegetable oils. What colour is it? Why do you think it is not colourless? Taste it. How would you describe its taste?

★★ **Activity.** Add a little olive (or other oil) to water in a test tube or bottle. Does the olive oil dissolve? Shake vigorously. What happens? Allow to settle. What happens? Do oils dissolve or mix with water?

26

Oils and fats are much more stable to heat than proteins. They can be heated to a temperature (Centigrade) two, or even three, times as great as that of boiling water before any change occurs.

★ ? If you wanted to cook food quickly (e.g. potatoes) would you choose hot fat or boiling water. Why?

VITAMINS

To some people vitamins seem rather mysterious things because they can't picture what they are like. If you feel like this, try the following activity.

★★ **Activity.** You can buy several vitamins at a chemists; one of the commonest is vitamin C which you can buy as tablets. What does a tablet of vitamin C look like? Crush one up in your mouth. What does it taste like?

You know now that at least one vitamin is not at all mysterious —it is simply a white solid with a rather pleasant sour taste. The other vitamins are not strange either; they are rather common-place solids or liquids like the other nutrients that go to make up our food, as you can see by checking the photograph on page 100.

Do you remember that carbohydrates, proteins and fats are each constructed according to a definite pattern? All fats, for example, are built up in the same way from fatty acids and glycerol. Members of the vitamin group, however, are not built up according to a common plan. Each vitamin is built up in a different way. They all contain the three elements carbon, hydrogen and oxygen, most contain nitrogen, and occasionally elements such as sulphur and phosphorus occur.

You may think it rather strange that we should put vitamins together into a single group, when they are really so different from each other. The reason for this is very simple. When vitamins were discovered nothing was known about how they were built. Until early in this century it was believed that a diet containing adequate amounts of carbohydrates, proteins, fats, mineral

27

elements and water would be sufficient for the maintenance of health. When such an artificial diet was tried out, however, it was found that it did not maintain health. The name of vitamin was therefore given to the group of substances which, when added in small amounts to the diet mentioned above, enabled it to maintain health.

★★★ **Keypoint.** Vitamins are essential to health but unlike proteins we only require very tiny amounts in our diet. Vitamins have been simply named after the letters of the alphabet A, B, C, etc.

MINERAL ELEMENTS

You are probably familiar with minerals, such as limestone and rock salt, that are dug out of the earth. You may be rather puzzled, however, to see any connection between them and the food that we eat. In fact the term mineral element is not a very good one to describe a group of nutrients because, for instance, we obviously cannot eat meals which form a part of natural minerals. The clue to the puzzle may be found in the last chapter. Though we cannot eat the mineral element sodium, we can eat sodium chloride,

The White Cliffs of Dover; could you eat them?

formed when sodium combines with chlorine. This is because the compound sodium chloride is quite unlike the sodium and chlorine from which it is made. In other words, while it is true to say that we must obtain mineral elements from our diet, it is not true to say that we eat the elements themselves. What we actually eat are the compounds which have been built from mineral elements. Thus by eating salt we obtain the mineral elements, sodium and chlorine.

We could even eat limestone—though it would not be very pleasant—and obtain another mineral element that we need, namely calcium. Indeed nowadays chalk, which is powdered limestone, is added to nearly all the flour from which our bread is made. This is done to ensure that we do not go short of calcium. It may strike you as strange to think that when you eat bread, you could be eating a little of the White Cliffs of Dover (see photo)— but it is true! Milk is one of the best sources of calcium in our diet.

Other examples of mineral elements that we must obtain from our food are *phosphorus, iron* and *iodine*. Although we need only small amounts of the last two, we could not live without them.

In addition to the mineral elements mentioned above, we need very tiny amounts of a number of others. The amounts that we need are so small—mere traces—that we call them *trace elements*. Though we need only such small amounts, we can no more do without trace elements than we can do without those, such as calcium, which we need in relatively large amounts. Iodine is a trace element and other examples are *manganese, zinc, cobalt* and *copper*. Since these elements are needed in such small amounts, we need not bother about which foods contain them. Almost any diet will supply us with more of these elements than we need.

★★★ **Keypoint.** Our food must supply us with the mineral elements we need, such as calcium, sodium, iron and iodine. We do not eat the elements themselves, however, but salts containing them.

★ ? In what forms do we eat (a) sodium and chlorine and (b) calcium and phosphorus?

3 Digestion and Enzymes

It's a very odd thing,
As odd as can be,
That whatever Miss T. eats,
Turns into Miss T.
De la Mare

It is indeed a very odd thing—a very remarkable thing—that no matter what we eat, it very soon becomes flesh and blood. There is little obvious similarity between the nature of the food we eat and the nature of our bodies. Indeed, the difference between them is so great that most of the food we eat is of no use to us at all until its nature has been completely changed. The process by which the nature of food is changed in the body is called *digestion*.

Many of the molecules found in food are very large as molecules go. You may remember, for example, that a large protein molecule may contain several hundred thousand atoms. Such molecules are far too large to be of use to the body. Before they can be used they must be broken down into molecules which are small enough to be *absorbed* into the bloodstream. After digestion food is absorbed into the blood in rather the same way that water is absorbed into a sponge. We can sum the matter up by saying that most of the nutrients of food cannot be used by our bodies until they have been digested and absorbed.

Let us begin by considering carbohydrates. One of the commonest forms of carbohydrate in food is starch. A starch molecule is large, being built up from a large number of glucose units. It is of no use to our bodies until it has been broken down into small soluble units that can be absorbed. This breakdown process occurs in stages; the starch molecule is broken down bit by bit until a molecule containing only two glucose units is left. This substance is maltose as we saw on page 16. However, the body cannot use

30

even this small molecule until it has been broken in half to form two glucose molecules. The result of this step-by-step breakdown process is that starch is completely converted into glucose.

We must next think of how this breakdown process occurs. It is fairly obvious that carbohydrate molecules do not simply fall apart when they are eaten, because the glucose units are firmly linked together. Some agent is needed to break the links between the glucose units. We shall get a clue to what happens from Fig. 8 on page 16, where the breakdown of sucrose is shown as being brought about by water, i.e. it is a hydrolysis. A solution of starch in water can also be hydrolysed and this may be done by boiling it with a little acid for a few minutes. After the water has broken all the links between the glucose units, we are left with a solution of glucose. The digestion of sucrose and starch in the body also takes place by hydrolysis.

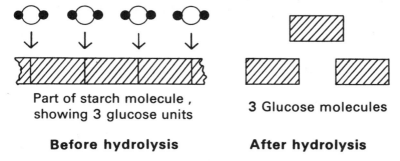

4 Water molecules

Part of starch molecule , showing 3 glucose units

3 Glucose molecules

Before hydrolysis   **After hydrolysis**

Fig. 12. The hydrolysis of starch into glucose

Just as starch molecules must be broken down into glucose molecules before they can be used by our bodies, so proteins must be broken down into amino acids. As we have seen, protein molecules consist of linked amino acid units, and in digestion the links which join the amino acid units are broken down step by step until each protein molecule has been completely converted into the amino acids from which it was built. The breakage of the links between amino acid units is brought about by hydrolysis.

Fats are also hydrolysed during digestion. Hydrolysis again takes place in stages, one fatty acid molecule being removed from a fat molecule in each stage. A fat molecule is sometimes called a

31

triglyceride, because *three* fatty acid molecules become joined to one *glycerol* molecule to form it. When one fatty acid molecule is split off from a fat molecule, the resulting molecule is called a *diglyceride* and if a further fatty acid molecule is removed a *monoglyceride* is formed. During digestion both monoglycerides and diglycerides are produced. The final stage, in which a monoglyceride is hydrolysed to glycerol, does not take place to any large extent. The first stage in the hydrolysis is shown in Fig. 13.

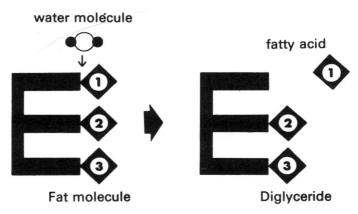

Fig. 13. The first stage in the hydrolysis of a fat molecule

★★★ **Keypoint.** Carbohydrates, proteins and fats need to be digested before they can be used in the body. In each case digestion involves the breakdown of a large molecule into many small ones. This process takes place in many steps. It is like starting with a large chain of beads and taking this to pieces by removing one bead at a time.

★ ? What is the name of the breakdown step in digestion? What does the name mean?

Not all nutrients need to be digested. Simple sugars, such as glucose, many vitamins and mineral salts and—of course—water, do not need to be broken down and can be absorbed into the body as they are.

32

Enzymes and digestion

We have seen that during digestion carbohydrates, proteins and fats are broken down into simple molecules by hydrolysis. We have also seen that hydrolysis cannot take place without water. But water itself is not enough. We cannot hydrolyse sucrose simply by making a solution of it in water; we must also add an acid. In the same way water alone is not enough to bring about hydrolysis in our bodies. In the stomach acid helps to bring about hydrolysis, but the main hydrolysing agents in the body are most important substances called *enzymes*.

★★★ **Keypoint.** Enzymes are proteins. Thousands of different enzymes are known, and they are all constructed out of large numbers of connected amino acid units. They are of vital importance in all the reactions going on in our bodies.

Enzymes which assist digestive processes are all involved in hydrolysis and so they are called *hydrolysing enzymes*. Later in the book we shall meet other types of enzymes which assist other sorts of reactions.

Enzymes as catalysts. Only a small quantity of a hydrolysing enzyme is needed to bring about the hydrolysis of a large amount of food. This is because although enzymes speed up hydrolysis, they are not used up in the process. Such substances are called *catalysts*. A catalyst may be likened to a moving escalator. If you climb an escalator that is not moving, it is a slow business. When the escalator is moving upwards, however, you can climb much more quickly, and when you step off at the top, the part you were standing on moves round again to the bottom. It is then available to carry someone else to the top. It is obvious that if you want to carry a large number of people up a stair quickly—as happens in the rush-hour on the London Underground—it is much better to use a moving escalator than a fixed stair.

There are two points to notice about an escalator. The first is that you use only the surface of the escalator, and the second is that after you have used the escalator it is still available for the use of other people. The catalytic action of an enzyme is rather similar. The enzyme acts by making its surface available to other substances, and for this reason it is called a *surface catalyst*.

In hydrolysis water reacts with some other substance, which we can call substance A. Before they can react, water and substance A must come together, and the enzyme surface is available to enable this to occur. If a molecule of substance A contains two units B and C linked together, hydrolysis breaks the link, so producing B and C as separate molecules. If substance A is sucrose, for example, B and C are glucose and fructose. After the new molecules have been formed, they move away from the enzyme surface, which is then ready to receive more molecules. In this way the enzyme surface can be used again and again, so that very little enzyme is needed to bring about the hydrolysis of a large number of molecules of A. This process is pictured in Fig. 14.

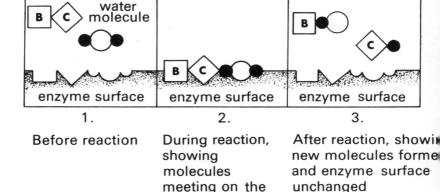

Fig. 14. How an enzyme catalyses hydrolysis

There is one way in which the action of an enzyme is quite different from that of an escalator. The escalator surface can be used by anyone, but an enzyme surface is so shaped that often it can be used by water and only *one* other substance. The reason for this will be clear from Fig. 14. Molecule A exactly fits the shape of the enzyme surface. You can compare enzyme hydrolysis to the fit of a key into a lock, with A acting as the key, and the enzyme as the lock. Only when the molecules of a substance fit into the enzyme surface can the enzyme act as a catalyst. The enzyme *lactase*, for example, acts as a catalyst to the sugar *lactose*, but it does not act as a catalyst to any other substance. This is like having

34

a burglar-proof lock, which can only be opened by one particular key.

The names of enzymes usually end in -*ase*. Thus the hydrolysis of *maltose* is catalysed by *maltase*, just as that of lact*ose* is catalysed by lact*ase*.

As each enzyme will only catalyse the hydrolysis of one particular substance—or of a group of substances which have molecules of a similar shape—a very large number of enzymes is needed for the digestion of food.

The importance of enzymes

Enzymes are vital to the process of digestion; they speed up the breakdown of food so that it is complete in a matter of hours. In a mere three or four hours huge molecules such as starch, containing perhaps 150 000 atoms have been broken down into quite small molecules containing only 24 atoms (simple sugars such as glucose). Without enzymes our bodies could not digest food; it is as simple as that.

We have stressed the importance of enzymes in digestion, but this is just one example of the many ways that enzymes affect us. One of the most familiar and earliest known processes controlled by enzymes is *fermentation*. Sugary solutions of fruit such as grape juice ferment quite naturally because they contain natural yeasts that hasten the breakdown of sugar into alcohol. At the same time carbon dioxide gas is produced:

$$\text{Sugar} + \text{enzymes in yeast} \longrightarrow \text{Alcohol} + \text{carbon dioxide}$$

It is the enzymes in the yeast which catalyse this change. If you are wondering where the yeast came from in the first place the answer is that the 'bloom' on the skin of a grape contains large numbers of tiny yeast cells and within these cells are a number of different enzymes that are responsible for fermentation. In fact this is how the name enzyme arose because it means literally 'in yeast'. If you turn to page 207 you will find out how the enzymes in yeast are involved in another important fermentation—in making bread.

★ ? When grape juice ferments what is the name of the alcoholic drink produced?

★★ Activity. Make up a sugar solution by dissolving about 10 g sugar in 100 ml water; also make a little (about 5 g) bakers' yeast into a paste with a little water and then add 50 ml water. Add the sugar solution and the yeast to a flask fitted with a tight cork and a glass U-tube, and leave it in a warm place (e.g. near a hot radiator). Note what happens (a) at once, and after (b) one day, (c) two days, (d) one week. If bubbles are being produced pass them into a tube of lime water (see page 49) and shake the flask. What happens? What is the gas produced? At the end of a week taste the contents of the flask. Describe the taste. Repeat the experiment, but keep the flask in a cold place. How does temperature affect the rate of the fermentation?

If wine is left for any length of time exposed to the air it turns sour because enzymes in bacteria present in the air change the alcohol into acetic acid or vinegar. While this would be unfortunate if it happened at home it is used on a large scale as the basis of making wine vinegar. In many countries wine is too expensive to

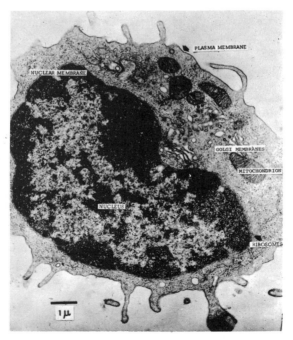

A typical human cell, magnified 20 000 times

be turned into vinegar and instead malt liquor is used, but it is made into malt vinegar by an enzyme process similar to that used in making wine vinegar.

Enzymes are important in many food-making processes (see Chapter 12 for further examples) but they are more than important in the body—they are vital. Without enzymes all life ceases; it is as drastic as that. The body is composed of some hundred thousand million cells, and these are so extremely tiny that it is only recently that we have been able to discover exactly what they are like using an instrument called an electron microscope. The photograph on page 36 shows a simple human cell magnified about 20 000 times. Although the cell is so small it is quite complicated as you can see from the photograph. Each cell can be likened to a factory which never stops production; there is ceaseless action involving large numbers of different activities. Each of these activities or reactions in every cell is controlled by its own set of enzymes. In the absence of the enzymes the activities of the cell would get completely out of control and we should die. You can perhaps picture each cell as a very busy road junction controlled by computer-controlled lights; without the lights chaos would result. The enzymes in the cell control the cell just as the lights control the junction; they decide what activities will take place and those that shall not.

★ ? How can you explain the fact that every cell in the body contains only very tiny amounts of enzymes, yet they manage to control all the activities of the cell?

★★★ **Keypoint.** Enzymes are proteins, and they act as catalysts, i.e. very small amounts only speed up reactions. Enzymes are highly selective; sometimes an enzyme will only speed up one particular reaction, so that in digestion, for example, many different enzymes are needed to break down proteins.

★★ **Activity.** List all the examples of enzyme action that you can think of.

Stages of digestion

The digestive system is really a very long tube—about 30 feet long in an adult—which is open at both ends. Food enters at the mouth, and passes slowly through the system being digested and absorbed on the way. Any food that is left is removed as waste from the other end of the tube, which is called the anus. The main parts of the digestive system are shown in Fig. 15.

Digestion begins as soon as food is eaten. The action of chewing food with our teeth breaks it into smaller pieces. These smaller pieces become mixed with a watery substance called *saliva*, which is produced by the *salivary glands*. Saliva moistens the food and makes it easier to swallow. It also contains a starch-splitting enzyme or amylase, which helps in the first stage of breaking down cooked starchy food. (*Amylase* is the general name given to any enzyme concerned with hydrolysing starchy foods.) The sight of

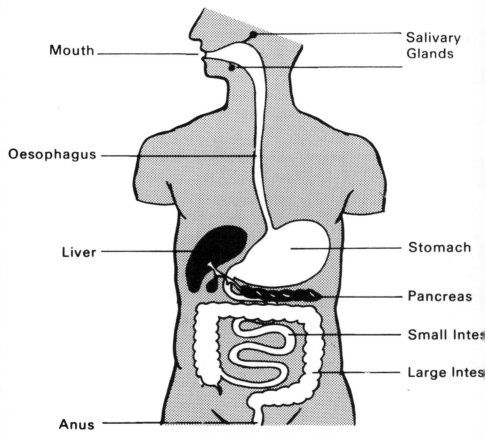

Fig. 15. The digestive system

a well-cooked meal, an appetizing smell or even the thought of a good meal aid digestion because they cause the salivary glands to produce plenty of saliva.

Food passes from the mouth into the oesophagus and is carried down it and into the stomach by gentle muscular action. Muscular action continues in the stomach and this causes food to become mixed with *gastric juice*, which is poured forth from the lining of the stomach. The appearance, smell and flavour of good food all help in ensuring a good flow of gastric juice. Gastric juice is an acidic watery liquid, which contains hydrochloric acid and a number of enzymes. The chief enzyme is *pepsin*, which catalyses the hydrolysis of proteins. Pepsin cannot assist in breaking all the links joining the amino acids in a protein molecule; indeed it can only break a few links, so in the stomach proteins are not broken down very much.

★★ **Activity.** Boil some egg white until it is solid and cut it into small pieces. Put a few pieces of egg white into two small beakers or similar containers and add about 10 ml of pepsin solution to each. Add to one container about 10 ml of water and to the other about 10 ml of 0·2% hydrochloric acid. Note what happens in each container. Why are the reactions in the two containers different? What does this experiment tell you about digestion in the stomach?

You will notice that not much digestion takes place in the stomach. The main purpose of the stomach is to prepare food for the main stage of digestion which takes place in the *small intestine*. This is a very long, narrow and coiled tube. As soon as food passes from the stomach into the upper part of the small intestine, digestive juices pour forth. *Pancreatic juice* comes from a gland called the *pancreas*, and contains a number of enzymes. It contains a protein-splitting enzyme or *peptidase* which continues the hydrolysis of proteins begun in the stomach. Pancreatic juice also contains an amylase which continues the breakdown of starch molecules begun in the mouth until maltose—containing only two glucose units—is formed. It also contains lipase, which causes partial hydrolysis of fat molecules. The name *lipase* is a general one for enzymes which help in the splitting of fat molecules.

★ ? Amylases, peptidases and lipases are all types of enzymes. How do they assist in digestion?

A second digestive juice called *bile* passes into the upper part of the small intestine. It comes from the liver, and though it contains no enzymes, it does contain salts. These convert fat (which is liquefied by the warmth of the stomach) into very small droplets, and this assists the action of fat-splitting enzymes, because a large surface area of fat is exposed to the enzyme surface.

The walls of the small intestine produce a digestive juice called *intestinal juice*. This contains enzymes which complete the hydrolysis of proteins into amino acids, and of starch into glucose.

The process of digestion is almost completed in the small intestine. Carbohydrates (except cellulose), proteins and fats are all in the form of small units, which are absorbed through the walls of the small intestine into the blood. Mineral elements, vitamins and water—which do not need to be broken down before they can be absorbed—are also absorbed at this stage.

Any food that has not been absorbed from the small intestine

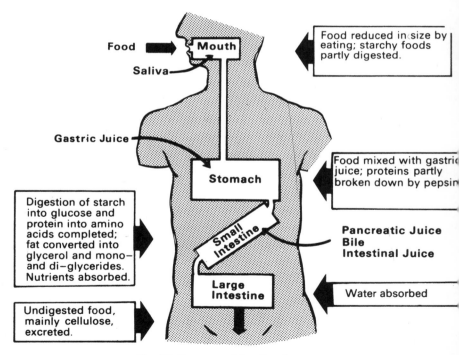

Fig. 16. Summary of the digestive process

passes into a wider and shorter tube called the *large intestine*. No new enzymes are produced here, and no further digestion takes place. The main task of the large intestine is to remove water from undigested material. All the breakdown stages in digestion are hydrolyses and therefore involve the use of water. A great deal of water passes into the digestive system in the form of digestive juices, and it is important to recover this so that it can be used again. Water is absorbed in the large intestine and passes back into the tissues. After the removal of water, undigested material is removed from the body through the anus.

Dietary Fibre. The undigested material consists of dietary fibre which, as we saw on page 19, cannot be digested by the body. Nevertheless it plays a very important role in maintaining health and preventing disease. Dietary fibre, and especially wheat fibre (bran), absorbs large amounts of water in the large intestine and its bulk increases by as much as twenty to thirty times. This is important because it makes the contents of the bowels soft and bulky; this makes stools easy to pass and prevents constipation. In the absence of fibre in our diet stools become small and hard and this makes them difficult to pass and causes constipation.

★ ? How many enzymes can you name that are involved in digestion? Can you say what each one does?

★ ? We can digest all carbohydrates except one. What is its name?

★★★ **Keypoint.** The stages of digestion are summarized in Fig. 16.

★★ **Activity.** Using the information given in Fig. 2 explain how the following meal is digested:

Fish and chips, bread and butter, an apple, white coffee with sugar.

4 Food and Energy

Measuring energy

Food supplies us with energy, and we are now going to see how we get energy from food and which foods give us the most energy. First, however, we must say a few words about measuring energy.

Energy may be measured as *heat*, and so we must be able to measure hotness. The degree of hotness of something is called its *temperature*. Temperature is measured with a thermometer, and is usually recorded in degrees *Celsius* (or Centigrade). On the *Celsius* scale we define the temperature at which water freezes at zero, and the temperature at which it boils as one hundred. We write these temperatures 0°C and 100°C. We also use the *Fahrenheit* scale, though this is going out of favour. On this scale the freezing point of water is 32 degrees (32°F) and the boiling point of water is 212 degrees (212°F). Both temperature scales are shown below.

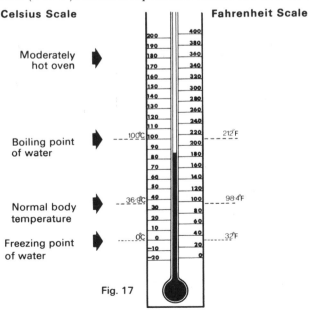

Fig. 17

Just as we need a definite unit of temperature—the degree—so we also need a definite unit of energy. The basic metric unit of energy (and work) is the *joule* (symbol J). 4·2 joules of heat energy are required to raise the temperature of 1 gramme of water by 1°C. The joule is too small a unit to be convenient for measuring the energy supplied by food, and so the kilojoule (kJ) is often used. This unit is one thousand times bigger than the joule, i.e. **1 kJ = 1000 J**. If you turn to Fig. 19 you will find the energy value of some typical foods expressed in kilojoules per gramme.

Although heat energy is now expressed in metric units (the joule or kilojoule) an older unit is still used. This is the kilocalorie, often abbreviated to Cal. Fortunately, it is easy to convert one unit into the other using the following conversion:

4·2 kilojoules = 1 kilocalorie

★★★ **Keypoint.** Remember that a kilocalorie is about four times as big as a kilojoule. So as an approximation to convert Cal to kJ multiply by 4; and to convert kJ to Cal divide by 4.

★ ? How much energy is needed to raise the temperature of 10 kilogramme of water by 1°C? Express your answer in kJ and Cal.

(Answer: 42 kJ, 10 Cal.)

Energy needed to sustain life

★ ? Why do our bodies need energy even when we are 'doing nothing' (e.g. sleeping in bed)? Turn to page 2 if you are not sure.

The energy needed to keep all our internal processes going is called the energy of *basal metabolism*, and you will find it discussed further on page 113. The energy of basal metabolism varies from person to person. Big people use up more energy than small people, men use up more than women and young people use up more than old. As an example, a young man of average build has a basal metabolism of about 7000 kilojoules per day.

Energy needed for physical activities

When we get up in the morning the rate at which we use up energy suddenly increases. Dressing, washing, going downstairs, eating

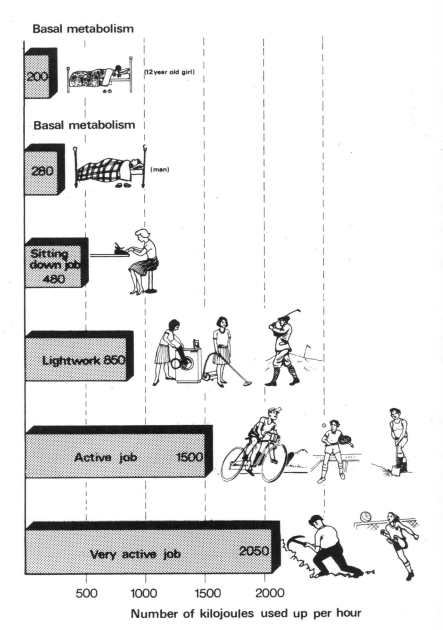

Basal metabolism

200 (12 year old girl)

Basal metabolism

280 (man)

Sitting down job 480

Lightwork 850

Active job 1500

Very active job 2050

500 1000 1500 2000

Number of kilojoules used up per hour

Fig. 18. The way energy needs vary with type of job

44

breakfast—all use up energy. In fact *every* physical activity uses up energy. Even if we are lazy for a day we use up a large amount of energy; and if we are energetic—and perhaps play netball or go for a swim—we use up an even larger amount.

In a similar way, people with energetic jobs, such as miners and farmers, use up larger numbers of joules than people who sit at their work, such as typists and bus drivers. The chart shown in Fig. 18, shows that the more active a job is, the greater is the amount of energy used. The figures given are only average values, as they vary from person to person. For instance, a fat man uses up more energy in doing a particular job than does a thin person, and a woman uses up rather less than a man.

★★ **Activity.** Using Fig. 18 work out how many kilocalories are used up per hour for each example given.

Using the sort of information given in Fig. 18 it is quite simple to work out our energy needs for a whole day. As an example let us work out how much energy a girl of 12 might use up on a typical day at school.

Activity	Hours	kJ/hour	kJ used up
Sleep	10	200	2 000
School life	6	480	2 880
Home life	6	500	3 000
Walking	1	1 200	1 200
Tennis	1	1 500	1 500
			10 580

In a day such a girl would use up between ten and eleven thousand kilojoules. You can compare this with a baby less than a year old who uses about 3000 kJ/day and a very active young man doing a lot of swimming or athletics who would need about 15 000 kJ/day.

Energy value of foods

Our energy needs must be supplied by food, and the amount of energy supplied by a food is called its *energy value*. We can express

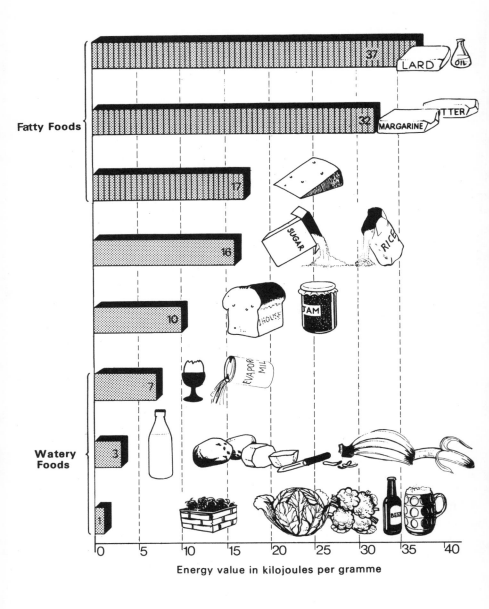

Fatty Foods

Watery Foods

Energy value in kilojoules per gramme

Fig. 19. The energy value of some foods

46

the energy value of a food as the number of kilojoules that a given weight of the food will make available to our bodies.

The three types of nutrient which provide us with energy are carbohydrates, fats and proteins. We can give to each of these an average energy value, and these are shown below:

Nutrient	Average energy value	
	Cal/g	kJ/g
Carbohydrate	4	16
Fat	9	37
Protein	4	17

If we eat a certain amount of fat it will give us more than twice as much energy as the same weight of carbohydrate or protein. This means that fatty foods—such as butter and cheese—are more concentrated sources of energy than mainly carbohydrate or protein foods such as potatoes and meat. Incidentally the difference in energy value between a hot meal and a cold meal is very small indeed compared with the energy value of the food itself.

Figure 19 shows the energy values of a number of foods. You will notice that fatty foods head the list, while foods containing a high proportion of water (which has no energy value), such as milk and strawberries, come at the bottom. You will find another way of comparing the energy values of foods illustrated in Fig. 40 on page 128. In this diagram you can see the amounts of different foods you would have to eat to gain 420 kilojoules.

If you turn back to Fig. 2 on page 7, you will see that carbohydrates and fats have only one function, to provide us with energy. Proteins, on the other hand, are concerned with all the three functions of food. In fact the *main* purpose of protein foods is to act as body-builders, and so we shall discuss them separately in the next chapter.

If you find it hard to visualize a gramme you may find it useful to look at the energy values of food in terms of amounts that are familiar to you. This is done in the table overleaf.

★★ **Activity.** In the table overleaf the column headed 'Cal' has been left blank. Can you fill it in?

Food	Amount	Weight (g)	kJ	Cal
Apple	one, large	150	300	
Cabbage	portion	100	100	
Beer	glass ($\frac{1}{2}$ pint)	300	300	
Milk	cup	150	450	
Egg	one medium	50	350	
Bread	one thick slice	45	450	
Jam	one tablespoon	45	450	
Cheese	one portion	20	340	
Sugar	four teaspoons	20	320	
Butter	for one slice of bread	15	480	

Energy from food

We talk of people being 'full of energy' meaning that they lead very active lives—perhaps, for example, they are enthusiastic swimmers or tennis players. The term 'full of energy' is not used in a scientific sense therefore, but as a general description of a person's behaviour. It bears no relation at all to the scientific use of the term energy. Thus an energy food is one which upon being eaten, digested and absorbed by the body provides the body with energy. To describe a food as being 'full of energy' is completely misleading. Food does not *contain* energy and therefore cannot be full of energy. Also the suggestion that any food can make us feel 'full of energy' is equally misleading and should be avoided.

The way food supplies us with energy

We obtain energy from food by *oxidizing* it. Oxidation can be thought of in a very simple way as the reaction of a substance with *oxygen*. In a car engine we have a similar type of reaction; petrol reacts with oxygen to produce a large amount of energy. This reaction happens so rapidly that it is really a small explosion. In our bodies the oxidation takes place much more slowly, but it is exactly the same *sort* of reaction.

Oxygen is brought into our bodies through the lungs and is carried round in the blood. Also in the blood is a small amount of dissolved *glucose*. Glucose is the basic source of human energy, and is produced during digestion of carbohydrate foods (except cellu-

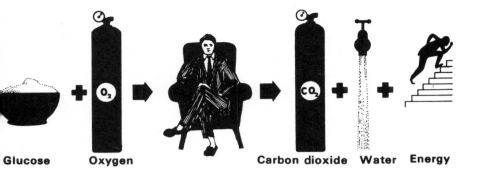

| Glucose | Oxygen | | Carbon dioxide | Water | Energy |

Fig. 20. The reaction of glucose with oxygen inside our bodies

lose). Glucose and oxygen react together producing carbon dioxide, water and energy (Fig. 20).

As we need energy all the time, this reaction between glucose and oxygen never stops. This means that our bodies are constantly producing carbon dioxide and water (as vapour), and these gaseous waste products are removed from our bodies through the lungs.

You can sometimes see the water present in breath. When you breathe out on a cold frosty morning you can see the little cloud of water droplets that is formed when the water vapour from your breath is turned into water by the drop in temperature.

There is also a simple test for carbon dioxide; when it is bubbled through a clear solution of *lime water*, the solution turns milky.

★★ **Activity.** Blow into a tube dipping into a solution of lime water Does it turn milky? If so what does it prove?

You may be wondering how this reaction between glucose and oxygen is slowed down in our bodies so that we obtain a controlled supply of energy. The answer is that the process is controlled by enzymes called *oxidizing enzymes*. You will remember that in digestion, the process of hydrolysis takes place in a number of steps, and that each step is controlled by a hydrolysing enzyme. In the

49

same way the reaction between glucose and oxygen takes place in a number of steps, each step being controlled by an oxidizing enzyme. As each step results in the release of a small amount of energy, the body receives the even flow of energy which it needs.

IMPORTANT ENERGY FOODS

Butter and margarine

We have already noted that fatty foods are the most concentrated sources of energy in our diet. You will notice from Fig. 19 (page 46) that margarine has a high energy value; that of butter is about the same. Both butter and margarine are therefore equally valuable as energy foods. At present we eat more margarine than butter (the actual proportions depend very much on their relative prices) but together they form an important part of our diet, supplying us with about one quarter of our total fat intake.

Butter is an animal fat made from cow's milk. Milk contains small droplets of oil, which rise to the surface when milk is kept and form the familiar 'cream layer'. Butter is made from cream which has been allowed to sour or 'ripen'. The sour cream is stirred or 'churned' until the oil drops have formed solid lumps of butter. The solid is removed from the liquid part—called butter milk—and salt and often colouring are added. The butter is then worked until a suitable consistency is obtained. You can follow the main stages of butter manufacture from the photographs on page 53.

Butter has been a part of the British diet for centuries. Indeed it is hard to imagine our diet without it. During the last century the demand for animal fats—of which butter and lard are the most common—increased so fast that production could not keep pace with demand. There was no shortage of liquid vegetable oils, however, and a way of converting liquid oils into solid fats was sought and discovered at the beginning of the present century.

The conversion of liquid oils into solid fats is called *oil hardening*, and it is done by a process called *hydrogenation*. The difference between oils and fats is due to the difference in the amounts of unsaturated fatty acid units that they contain (page 26). Oils contain more of such acid units than fats. To convert an oil into a fat, therefore, we must change the *unsaturated* fatty acids into *saturated*

50

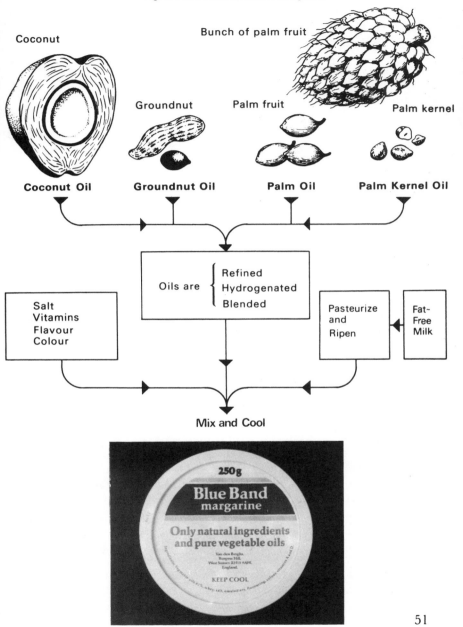

Fig. 22. The manufacture of margarine

Two sources of vegetable oil used for making margarine. *Left*. Cotton. *Right*. Oil palm

ones. This can be done by reacting the oil with hydrogen. The reaction is slow at room temperature, but it can be speeded up by pumping in the hydrogen under pressure and warming the oil in the presence of a small amount of the metallic element, *nickel*. Nickel is a catalyst and so helps to speed up the reaction.

★★★ **Keypoint.** Hardening of oils:

$$\text{Liquid oil} + \text{hydrogen} \xrightarrow[\text{heat}]{\text{nickel catalyst}} \text{solid fat}$$

Margarine is an important fat made by hydrogenation of oils. The oils used are usually a mixture of animal, vegetable and marine oils though some are purely vegetable. The actual mixture used varies from time to time according to the cost but typical ones used are:

Animal fat: lard.
Vegetable oils: soya bean, oil palm (see photo), cotton (see photo), groundnut, coconut.
Marine oils: anchovy, herring.

The oils are blended together, refined and hydrogenated. The hydrogenated oils are mixed with ripened milk, from which the cream has been removed. An emulsifying agent—which aids the formation of an emulsion—is added and mixing is continued until an emulsion (see p. 78) which looks like thick white cream is obtained. On cooling, the emulsion becomes solid, and this is worked until it has a smooth even texture.

One advantage of margarine over butter is that it has a much

Butter Manufacture. (1) Cream passes through pasteurizers (background) into large tanks (foreground) where it is allowed to ripen. (2) Cream is churned in rotating vessels and forms a granular solid. (3) When the butter is of the proper consistency it is removed from the churn. (4) The butter is packed in automatic machines

wider *plastic range*, i.e. it remains soft and can be spread over a wide range of temperature. Margarine can be made as hard or soft as desired, and nowadays you can buy soft margarine that spreads easily in summer and winter and easily 'creams' for making cakes (see page 210).

In order to improve the flavour of margarine and make it as similar as possible to butter, various substances are added to it during its manufacture. Flavouring agents and salt are added to try and produce a butter flavour and a yellow dye is added to give it a butter colour. Also, vitamins A and D are added in such quantities that margarine contains at least as much of these vitamins as butter.

The nutritional value of margarine is about the same as that of butter. They are both about four-fifths fat and one-fifth water and in addition they both contain valuable amounts of vitamins A and D. Margarine is as good a food as butter and it may be better, because it has a fixed vitamin content, whereas that of butter varies, being higher in summer than in winter.

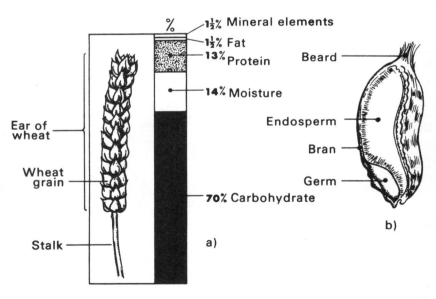

Fig. 23. (a) The composition of wheat and (b) the structure of a wheat grain (as a section through the germ)

54

Wheat and milling

Of all the cultivated grasses known as *cereals*, wheat is the most important in Britain. Wheat is now grown in most parts of the world, from tropical regions such as India to temperate regions such as the prairies of Canada, and even to the cold areas bordering on the Arctic Circle.

When wheat is threshed the wheat *grains* are separated from the stalks and the chaff. An average grain of wheat is about a quarter of an inch long and an eighth of an inch broad. As you can see from Fig. 23 a wheat grain is roughly egg-shaped, with a number of small hairs, called the *beard*, at one end. There are three main parts of a wheat grain; the seed or *germ*, the *endosperm* which makes up over 80% of the grain, and a tough outer skin called the bran.

THE MAIN PARTS OF A WHEAT GRAIN

Part of grain	Description	Per cent of whole	Composition
Endosperm	Food reserve for germ	80–85	Mainly starch, also contains some protein
Bran	Tough outer coat; brown colour	13–17	Mainly fibre; also contains B vitamins and minerals
Germ	Seed or embryo	2–3	Rich in fat, protein, B vitamins, vitamin E and iron

The main parts of a grain of wheat are indicated in the table above, from which it can be seen that the outer layer of bran consists mainly of indigestible fibre. The germ is rich in a variety of nutrients while the endosperm is mainly starch, the spaces between the starch grains being filled with protein.

★ ? Why do you think that the bran is usually removed from wheat grains before they are used as food? Try and find out why some people sprinkle bran on to certain foods (see also page 71).

55

The actual composition of different types of wheat varies a good deal, but average values are given in Fig. 23. You will see from these figures that the main nutrient in wheat is carbohydrate, and for this reason wheat is usually regarded as an energy food. Indeed, food products made from wheat provide most people with about one-fifth of their energy needs (see also page 63).

Whole grains of wheat being difficult to digest because of their outer cellulose layer, it is usual to remove the bran and convert the grains into a powdery flour before they are used as food. This process is known as *milling*, and in essence it consists of removing the bran and germ, and grinding the endosperm into powder with rollers. The actual process is very complex, however, and we shall only be able to give a brief outline of it here.

Before milling starts different varieties of wheat are blended together in such a way that the resulting flour has the properties needed for the purpose for which it is to be used. It is then cleaned, so that small stones, dust, chaff and so on are removed. In the first

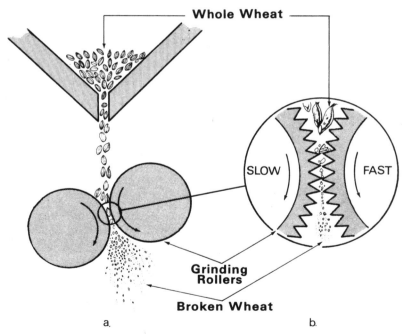

Fig. 24. The first stage of milling showing how the grain is broken down by shearing as it passes between the rollers

stage of milling the wheat grains are passed through a series of rollers with corrugated surfaces. The rollers are arranged in pairs and the rollers of each pair rotate in opposite directions and at different speeds (see Fig. 24). As the grains pass between the rollers, they are torn open and the endosperm released. Each pair of rollers is set closer together than the preceding pair, so that the endosperm is ground into increasingly small particles. The branny material is removed by sieving, and the endosperm is passed through a series of smooth rollers which convert it into a fine powder. Finally the powder is sieved and this removes the germ, which is flattened, rather than powdered, by the smooth rollers.

Types of flour and bread

The milling process can be modified to give more or less flour from a given amount of wheat. The percentage of flour obtained is called the *extraction rate* of the flour. For example, true *wholemeal* flour has an extraction rate of 100%, meaning that the whole grain has been converted into flour. It gets its brown colour from a pigment in the bran. As the extraction rate is lowered, the proportion of bran remaining in the flour decreases and so the colour becomes lighter and the flour more digestible. A typical white flour in use to-day has an extraction rate of 70% and such a flour contains almost nothing but crushed endosperm.

★ ? Starting from 200 grammes of wheat how much wheat flour will you get if the extraction rate is (a) 100%, (b) 80% and (c) 70%. Which contains the least bran?

The table overleaf summarizes the main types of wheat flour in common use; we shall say more about some of them later.

As the extraction rate goes down, so does the amount of vitamins and mineral elements in the flour. The proportion of bran and germ in the resulting flour is also reduced. Thus such flour contains less mineral elements (particularly iron) and vitamins (particularly vitamins of the B group) than flour of a higher extraction rate. It also contains somewhat reduced amounts of protein and calcium.

White bread or brown? In view of these facts you may wonder why we normally eat bread made from white flour rather than from wholemeal or brown flour. The real reason why we do this is that we prefer a white loaf to a dark-coloured loaf. Since very early times white bread has been a symbol of prosperity. As far back as Roman times white bread was eaten by rich people of the towns, whereas the poorer countryfolk had to be content with the cheaper wholemeal loaf. Thus white bread was prized because it was an expensive luxury; also because most people associated whiteness with purity. Nowadays we do not regard white bread as a luxury— indeed we take it for granted—but we still tend to feel that a fine white flour is 'purer' than a coarse brown one.

TYPES OF WHEAT FLOUR

Name	Description	Use
Wholemeal	100% extraction	Wholemeal bread
White flour	70% extraction	White bread
Strong	Contains more than 10% protein	Bread
Weak or soft	Contains less than 10% protein	Cakes and biscuits
Self-raising	Flour plus baking powder	Suitable for plain cakes and scones
Starch-reduced	Flour minus a proportion of the starch	Bread for slimming
Wheatgerm	Flour enriched by addition of wheat germ	Proprietary breads such as *Hovis*
Granary	Wheatmeal flour plus malted grains of barley and rye	Granary bread

See how many of these different types of loaves and rolls you can identify

★★★ **Keypoint.** The advantages of wholemeal flour over white flour are that vitamins, mineral elements and dietary fibre (as bran) are not lost in milling. Wholemeal flour contains all the fibre of the original wheat grain while white flour contains only one-third.

Although wholemeal flour contains more mineral elements, vitamins and fibre than white flour the nutrients in wholemeal flour may not be so well absorbed into the body as white flour. This is because there is more of a substance called *phytic acid* in brown flour than in white. Phytic acid combines with calcium and iron in the flour to form insoluble salts which the body cannot absorb. Luckily some of the phytic acid in flour is broken down during baking, and so the loss of nutrients due to this cause is not very great.

What we have just said will suggest to you that the superiority of wholemeal flour over white is not so obvious as it seemed at first sight. However, the fact remains that during the milling of white flour, nutrients are lost. For this reason certain nutrients are now added to all flour in Great Britain—except 100% wholemeal—to make good the losses that occur during milling. The vitamins *thiamine* and *nicotinic acid*, and the mineral elements *iron* and *calcium* (in the form of chalk) are added in sufficient quantities to ensure that the amounts present will be equivalent to the amounts in flour of 80% extraction rate. In the case of calcium the amount present will greatly exceed that in such 80% flour. In fact there is enough calcium to react with all the phytic acid present *and* leave some over for us!

★ ? Name the advantages of wholemeal bread compared with white bread. Can you think of any disadvantages? Which do you prefer?

★ ? What nutrients are added to white flour in Great Britain? Why are they added?

Breadmaking

If you think for a moment of a freshly-baked loaf of bread with its delicious smell, its light open texture and its crisp brown crust, you will realize that great changes occur when bread is made from flour.

60

Bread is made from flour, water, yeast and salt. There are many ways in which these ingredients can be converted into bread; one way of doing this on a large scale is shown on page 62. In this traditional method the dough formed when flour and water are mixed together is aerated by fermentation. In a more modern method, known as the *Chorleywood Process*, the long fermentation is replaced by a short period of very rapid mixing. At the same time vitamin C is added to improve the dough. This new method is much quicker than the old and in Great Britain most bread made on a large scale is now made by this process.

We shall say more about the principles of bread-making in Chapter 11.

More and more bread is being made in factories and we are now familiar with factory-made bread which has lost its crisp brown crust and has a standard shape and texture and often comes sliced and wrapped. However, much bread is still made by the small baker who makes a wide variety of different types of loaf, some of which are shown on page 59.

★★ **Activity.** Carry out a survey of your local bread shops and list the different types of loaves and rolls made from white flour. Give a brief description of the appearance of each.

★★ **Activity.** See how many different types of bread you can find in your local shops, e.g. white, wholemeal, malt. List them all and try and find out the main differences between them.

Bread as a food

Most people think of bread as a useful source of starch or as a 'good' carbohydrate food. They regard bread as an energy food and think that apart from this it is not a very valuable part of the diet. How wrong they are! It is true, of course, that wheat is mainly carbohydrate as you can see by turning back to Fig. 23. But you will also notice that it contains smaller amounts of other nutrients and you will remember that certain vitamins and mineral elements are added to all flour except wholemeal to replace losses that occur during milling. Although bread consumption in Great Britain is steadily going down we still eat on average nearly three small loaves a week each. This is quite a lot of bread and it means that bread contributes quite a proportion of the nutrients in our diet apart from carbohydrate.

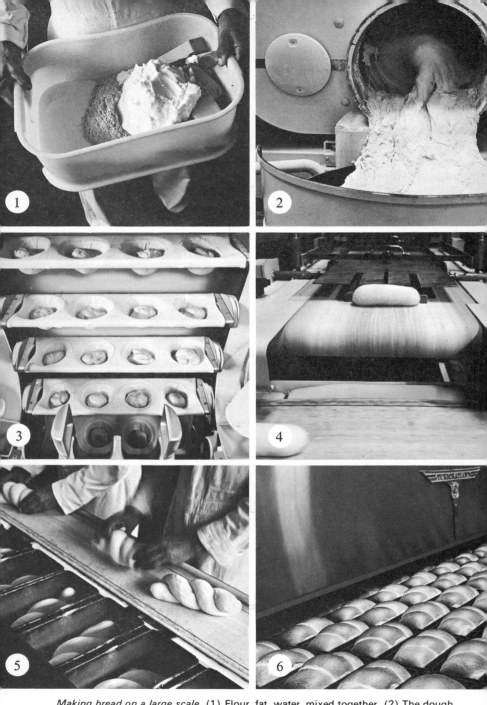

Making bread on a large scale. (1) Flour, fat, water, mixed together. (2) The dough is taken from the mixer and (3) rolled into balls and allowed to ferment. (4) It is cut again, (5) twisted, put into greased tins and proved again. (6) It moves through the oven and is cooked

★★★ **Keypoint.** Bread contributes the following to an average diet:

15% of the energy; 16% of the protein; 19% of the iron; 13% of the calcium; 22% of the vitamin B_1.

★★★ **Keypoint.** We usually think of eggs and cheese as good protein foods (see Fig. 2), and yet because we eat so much bread it provides us with more protein than eggs and cheese **combined**.

★★★ **Keypoint.** We usually think of milk as our chief source of calcium. This is true but bread is our second most important source.

★★★ **Keypoint.** In terms of value for money, bread is still one of the 'best buys' in terms of nutritional value.

★ ? Bread is sometimes called a staple food. What does this mean?

COMPARISON OF CEREALS

	Form in which cereal is used for food	Energy value in kJ/g	Cooked forms	Manufactured food products
Wheat	Wheat flour (white)	11	Bread, buns, cakes, biscuits	Bread, semo-lina, Puffed Wheat, Grape-nuts
Oats	Oatmeal	17	Parkin, porridge, oat-cakes	Breakfast cereals, e.g. Oat Crunchies
Rye	Rye flour	14	Rye bread	Rye bread, Ryvita
Barley	Pearl barley	15	Added to some soups and stews	Malt, barley water
Maize	Maize flour	15	Corn-on-the-cob	Corn flakes, cornflour, custard and blancmange powders
Rice	Rice flour (groundrice), Polished rice	15	Rice puddings, savoury rice dishes	Breakfast cereals, e.g. Rice Crispies

Other cereals

Although wheat is the most important cereal eaten in countries with a temperate climate rice is the most widely used in tropical countries. Indeed rice is the staple food of about half the world's population. The energy value and uses of cereals are summarised in the table on page 63.

Cereals play an important part in the British diet. Between them they provide more than one-third of our energy needs. In addition they supply us with valuable amounts of protein, calcium, iron and B vitamins.

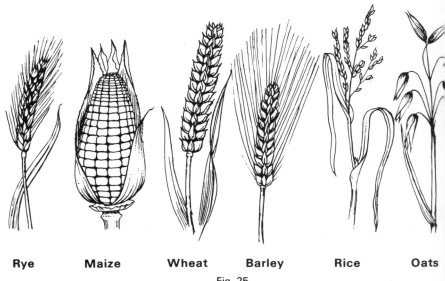

Rye   Maize   Wheat   Barley   Rice   Oats

Fig. 25

Potatoes

Potatoes are so much a part of our everyday diet, that it comes as rather a surprise to learn that they were only introduced into England towards the end of the sixteenth century. Even more surprising is the fact that the people of England were so suspicious of them that they did not become a normal part of our English diet until another two hundred years had passed. Nowadays it is unusual for a day to go by when we do *not* eat potatoes during at least one of our meals.

When potatoes are growing the only part that is visible is the

64

green leafy part. It is here that the plant manufactures its food supply, which consists mainly of starch. The potato is classified as a *tuber* because this food material is stored in a swollen stem or tuber which develops underground. When we eat potatoes, we are really eating the reserve food supply of the plant.

Potatoes contain about 15% to 20% starch, the remainder being mainly water together with small amounts of proteins, mineral elements and vitamins. Potatoes are mainly prized as an energy food, though their energy value is only 3 kJ/g. If you refer back to Fig. 19 on page 46 you will see that this is a low value, and that bread, for example, provides about three times as much energy as an equal weight of potatoes. Nevertheless, if we eat

% Composition

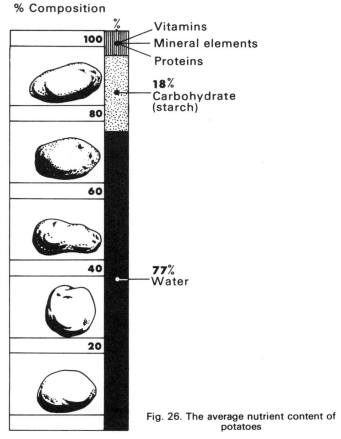

Fig. 26. The average nutrient content of potatoes

large quantities of potatoes they are a useful source of energy—and also of proteins.

Potatoes contain only small amounts of vitamins, the main one being vitamin C (ascorbic acid). When potatoes are peeled and cooked, some of the vitamin C is lost, yet in spite of this potatoes supply an average person with nearly one quarter of his total intake of this vitamin. Potatoes also contain small amounts of the vitamins thiamine and nicotinic acid, and the mineral element iron.

★★★ **Keypoint.** Although potatoes are mainly water and starch it is not correct to think of them only as an energy food. We eat such large quantities—about 1 kg per week—that they supply us with useful amounts of protein and vitamin C.

★★★ **Keypoint.** Potatoes are the most important source of vitamin C in the diet. In winter when fresh vegetables and fruit are in short supply they provide us with half our intake of vitamin C.

★ **?** Blackcurrants contain ten times as much vitamin C as potatoes, yet they provide us with a tiny proportion of our intake of this vitamin, whereas potatoes provide one-third of our intake. How do you explain this?

Other vegetables

Vegetables, other than potatoes, are poor energy foods, but they are useful sources of vitamins, particularly of vitamins A and C. For example, root vegetables such as carrots are valuable sources of vitamin A, green vegetables such as cabbage and sprouts provide us with vitamins A and C, and pulses such as peas and beans contain vitamin A and some B vitamins. Bulbs, such as onions and leeks, have very little nutritional value (see Table). Most vegetables, but especially peas, beans and lentils, are good sources of dietary fibre.

★★ **Activity.** See if you can name the vegetables shown in the photograph on page 67. Which of them has (a) the highest energy value and (b) the highest content of vitamin A?

Sugar

Sugar may be extracted either from sugar-*beet* or from sugar-*cane*, but whichever source is used, the product obtained is the same.

Sugar-cane, which grows only in tropical countries, is a type of giant grass. It resembles bamboo and may grow as high as 6 metres. Sugar-beet, which grows in temperate climates such as that of Great Britain, has a large white-pink root in which the sugar is stored.

TYPES OF VEGETABLE AND THEIR NUTRIENT CONTENT

Type	Examples	% Carbo-hydrate	% Pro-tein	% Fat	Vitamins
Green Leaves	Cabbage	6	2	0	A and C
	Lettuce	2	1	0	a little C
	Sprouts	5	4	0	A and C
Roots and Tubers	Carrot	5	1	0	Rich in A
	Turnip	4	1	0	C
	Beetroot	10	2	0	Traces only
Bulbs	Onions	5	1	0	Very little C
Fruits and Seeds	Peas	11	6	0	Some A, B and C
	Runner beans	3	1	0	A and C
	Tomatoes	3	1	0	A and C
Leaf stalks	Celery	1	1	0	traces only
Flower buds	Cauliflower	3	3	0	C

A selection of vegetables

Contrasts in harvesting sugar cane. *Top:* Cutting by hand (Jamaica). *Bottom:* Mechanical harvesting (Australia)

Sucrose is extracted from sugar cane by crushing the cane and spraying it with water. The solution obtained contains the sucrose and also some impurities. The impurities are removed by boiling the solution, adding lime and filtering. The clear solution which is left is concentrated until a mixture of sugar crystals and liquid—called *molasses*—is formed. The liquid is removed by spinning the mixture in a machine rather like a spin drier. It consists of a drum containing holes, through which the liquid escapes. If sugar beet is the starting material, the procedure is similar, except that the sucrose is extracted from the beet by shredding it, and by steeping the shredded beet in hot water.

Raw sugar, whether obtained from cane or beet, still contains some impurities and these are removed in the next part of the process. The raw sugar is redissolved in water, and carbon dioxide is bubbled through the solution and lime added to remove impurities. The resulting brownish solution is decolourized by passing it through a bed of charcoal, and concentrated by heating in 'vacuum pans'. During the concentration process sugar crystals form, and the liquid is removed by spinning as before. The liquid, which is rich in sugar, is used for making golden syrup or brown sugar.

Sugar in crystalline form as obtained by the above method is almost pure sucrose, the nature and properties of which were discussed in Chapter 2. In addition to normal granulated sugar, other types are produced and graded according to crystal size. *Lump sugar* is a form of granulated sugar in which the crystals are bound together in a solid mass. The mass is cut into cubes of any desired size by machines, any fragments being sold as *preserving sugar*. *Caster sugar* contains smaller crystals than granulated sugar, and *icing sugar* contains even smaller crystals, obtained by grinding granulated sugar to a powder.

★ ? Is there any difference between cane sugar and beet sugar? Why is raw sugar brown?

Sugar and health

Until about 200 years ago ordinary people could afford to eat very little sugar; it was a luxury food enjoyed only by the rich. As the years have passed sugar has become cheaper and cheaper and consumption has gone up and up. During this century world consumption of sugar has increased threefold—yes, 300%! In Britain on average we each eat 40 kg of sugar each year. About half of this amount is bought by the housewife as sugar, and about half is used in manufactured goods, such as cakes, ice-cream and sweets. In Britain we eat more sweets per person than in any other country.

★★★ **Keypoint.** It is best to eat as wide a variety of foods as possible. If we eat too much of any one food this may cause our health to suffer, and sugar is no exception to this general rule. The simple truth is that we eat far too much sugar. Cutting down on sugar cannot possibly do any harm and is likely to be good for health. There are two particular reasons for eating less sugar.

First. Sugar is almost pure carbohydrate—it contains no other nutrient. Most people in Britain have enough, if not too much, carbohydrate in their diet. Many of us are too fat and the simplest way to become slimmer is to eat less carbohydrate. The best way to do this is to eat less of foods such as sugar that contain no other nutrient. For example, if we were to eat less bread we should certainly eat less carbohydrate, but we would also get less protein, mineral elements and vitamins than we need. If we eat too many sugar-rich foods we feel like eating less of the foods we really need.

Second. Sugar is bad for teeth. Carbohydrate foods in general, and sugar in particular, become lodged on the surface of teeth where they are acted on by enzymes in bacteria which convert them into acids. These acids attack the enamel of teeth and cause decay. Sticky foods—such as toffees, gooey cakes, porridge and suet puddings—which stay in contact with the teeth for a long time, produce most decay. Foods eaten between meals cause more decay than when eaten as part of a meal.

Keeping your mouth clean is an important part of personal hygiene and well worth the trouble. Careful brushing of teeth after meals, not eating between meals and chewing fibre-rich foods such as celery, carrots or an apple all help to prevent decay.

5 Body-building Foods

Do you sometimes check your height and weight? If you do you will know that your body is continually growing and therefore needs a plentiful supply of body-building material. When you are fully grown you will need a smaller supply of body-building nutrients, but you will still need enough to replace worn and damaged tissues and to build small amounts of new material, such as nails and hair.

Our bodies are made up of millions of tiny cells, and *every* cell contains *protein*. Protein is therefore one of the most important body-building nutrients. Groups of cells are built up into tissues, some of which are hard and some of which are soft. Bones and teeth are the most important hard tissues and are made of calcium phosphate built from oxygen and the mineral elements *calcium* and *phosphorus*. Muscle and nerve tissues are examples of soft tissues and these also contain mineral elements of which *iron, phosphorus* and *sulphur* are the most important.

It is clear that the main body-building nutrients are protein and some mineral elements (Fig. 27), though, as we shall see in the next chapter, they cannot always be used by the body without the assistance of vitamins, water and other mineral elements.

Protein quality

★ ? Are protein molecules large or small? What is the name of the small units of which proteins are made? (Turn back to page 21 if you are in doubt.) How would you describe a protein molecule?

About twenty different amino acids are found in protein molecules, though no single protein contains them all. If an adult is provided with *eight* of these amino acids in his food, his body can make the other amino acids that it needs for itself. A growing person needs *ten* of these amino acids, which are called *essential* amino acids.

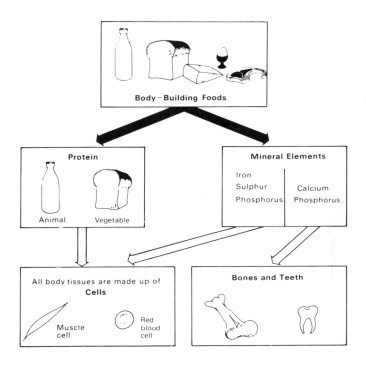

Fig. 27. Body-building foods are needed for the growth and maintenance of bone and tissues

Our diet *must* supply us with enough essential amino acids, because our bodies either cannot make them at all or cannot make them fast enough for our needs. It is clear that we must judge protein foods according as to whether they do or do not supply us with all the essential amino acids.

The quality of a protein can be found by feeding it to an animal or man and measuring the percentage of absorbed protein that is converted into body protein. The result is known as the *biological value* of the protein. For example egg protein contains all the essential amino acids and in the right amounts for the human body. All the protein of egg is therefore used for body building and it has a biological value of 100. On the other hand gelatin is completely lacking in one essential amino acid and if used on its own it would be useless for body building. It therefore has a biological value of 0.

Most proteins contain all the essential amino acids and proteins from animal sources have high biological value, i.e. the proportions of essential amino acids they contain are similar to those in the body. Most proteins of vegetable origin, on the other hand, have low biological value. There is a notable exception to this general rule in *soya beans* which have a biological value similar to that of animal protein.

★ ? How many mineral elements needed by the body can you name (without looking back!)?

★ ? Why are some amino acids called *essential*?

Animal and vegetable protein and the diet

A diet in which the only protein present was gelatin would be useless, because it would be completely lacking in one essential amino acid. However if gelatin is eaten with bread which is rich in the essential amino acid missing from gelatin, the mixture has a higher biological value than either on their own. This shows how important it is to eat protein of high and low biological value together.

If we ate nothing but vegetable protein (see vegetarian diet, page 144) we might well go short of some essential amino acids. This does not mean, of course, that vegetable protein is useless, but it does mean that vegetable protein should be eaten along with animal protein. In this way we receive a variety of different amino acids in the right sort of proportions for our body's needs.

Our bodies cannot store protein, and if they receive more than they need for body-building they use the remainder as a source of energy. It is therefore bad planning to have plenty of protein one day and none the next, because most of it will be used for energy, and we shall go short of protein for body-building. Diets should be planned so that *every* meal contains a proportion of protein and if possible about half of this should be animal protein. If the amount of animal protein available is limited, it should be spread out over as many meals as possible, and eaten with plenty of vegetable protein. Bread and cheese; milk and cereals; eggs and fish eaten with chips are all useful combinations, which provide a mixture of animal and vegetable protein.

It is important to get some idea of which foods are good sources of protein. In Fig. 28 you will see some of the most important protein foods in our diet. Each portion of food shown represents the amount needed to provide one-fifth the daily allowance of protein for a girl, twelve to fifteen years old. You should notice which foods have a high protein content (e.g. soya flour and cheese) and which have a low one (e.g. potatoes).

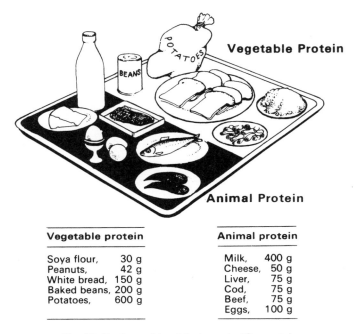

Vegetable protein		Animal protein	
Soya flour,	30 g	Milk,	400 g
Peanuts,	42 g	Cheese,	50 g
White bread,	150 g	Liver,	75 g
Baked beans,	200 g	Cod,	75 g
Potatoes,	600 g	Beef,	75 g
		Eggs,	100 g

Fig. 28. Portions of food that supply 12 g protein

The foods shown in Fig. 28 have been divided up into animal and vegetable protein, and this will remind you that in meal planning, protein of both types should be included. It will also remind you that although six slices of bread and one pint of milk contain the same *amount* of protein, the *value* of the milk protein for body-building is much greater than that of the bread.

★ ? Which of these dishes contains a balanced mixture of animal and vegetable protein? Macaroni cheese, ham and chips, fish and chips, beans and chips, bread and butter pudding.

★ **?** Why should protein form a part of each meal? Why is it better to have a little protein often rather than a large amount every now and then?

Mineral elements for body-building

Calcium and phosphorus are the two main mineral elements that we need for body-building. Phosphorus is present in a wide variety of foods, and any normal diet will supply our needs. Cheese, milk, meat, fish and oatmeal are all good sources of phosphorus. Calcium, on the other hand, is not present in large amounts in many foodstuffs, and proper diet planning is needed to ensure that we obtain enough. Milk and milk products are the best sources of calcium in our diet, and they supply well over half our total intake. Calcium is added to all flour (except wholemeal) in this country to make sure we do not go short of calcium. Thus bread, biscuits, cakes and all foods made from flour are good sources of calcium.

Food	
Milk,	300 g
Dried skimmed milk,	23 g
Cheese,	43 g
Sardines,	21 g
White flour,	230 g
Kippers,	300 g
Eggs,	600 g
White bread,	350 g

Fig. 29. Portions of food that supply 350 mg calcium

If you look at Fig. 29 you will see the amount of different foods needed to supply half the calcium allowance of a boy or girl aged nine to fifteen (350 mg). When you plan meals, you should include some of the foods shown each day so that our calcium needs are met.

★★★ **Keypoint.** Milk is the best source of calcium in our diet. All diets should include milk, preferably a pint daily. Milk is especially important for growing youngsters and women during pregnancy and when breast-feeding babies.

★★ Activity. Work out three ways in which a boy or girl aged nine to fifteen could obtain their calcium needs (700 mg) for a day, using the information given in Fig. 29. (You can express the amount of milk in grammes or pints. 1 pint of milk contains 680 mg calcium.)

IMPORTANT BODY-BUILDING FOODS

Milk and cheese; meat and fish; bread and other foods made from flour; eggs—these are the main body-building foods in our diet. In addition to being body-builders bread and flour are also important sources of energy, and as such were discussed in the last chapter.

Milk

Milk is one of our most valuable foods. When we talk of milk, we normally mean cow's milk and though we could not live on it alone—it is not a *perfect* food—it is nevertheless a rich source of nutrients.

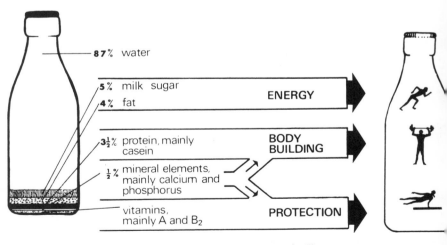

Fig. 30. The nutrient content of milk

The nutrient content of milk is shown in Fig. 30, and you will notice that it contains every class of nutrient. In spite of this, milk is nearly nine-tenths water and you might be tempted to class it with drinks, such as fruit squash or tea. However, this would be a great mistake! Milk is much more than a pleasant drink, because the 13% of solid material that it contains supply us with valuable nutrients in their most digestible form.

Milk as a body-builder. Milk is prized mainly as a body-building food. If you turn back to Figs. 28 and 29 you will note the importance of milk as a source of protein and calcium. It also supplies useful amounts of phosphorus. But the body-building value of milk is even greater than these figures suggest. The quantity of protein in milk is not great but what it lacks in quantity it makes up for in quality. All the proteins in milk are of high biological value, the most important being *casein*. This is a conjugated protein (see page 24) containing phosphorus. In addition milk proteins are easily digested, so that little is lost through incomplete digestion.

During digestion milk becomes solid, because in the stomach an enzyme called *rennin* coagulates casein into a hard clot. You can make milk clot very easily yourself.

★★ **Activity.** Warm a little milk to about blood-heat (36°C) and add a few drops of *rennet* (a preparation containing rennin). Allow to cool and leave until some solid has formed. Remove a little solid (the milk clot). Taste a little, test a little with litmus paper to see if it is acid or alkali (litmus turns red with acid, blue with alkali), and burn a little noting the smell (when proteins burn the smell is that of singed hair). Test the liquid, called whey, with litmus and note its colour.

Note. In this experiment you have really made *junket*, an easily digested and nutritious pudding.

Energy nutrients in milk. You know that when milk is allowed to stand for a time a layer of cream forms at the top. The fat in milk is in the form of very tiny droplets. They are so small that a single drop of milk contains several million of them. When milk is shaken the oil drops become dispersed through the milk, but on standing the oil drops rise to the surface and form a layer. Such a mixture of droplets dispersed in another liquid is called an *emulsion* (other well-known emulsions are mayonnaise, salad dressings and creamed cake mixes). The fact that milk fat is in the form of an emulsion makes it very easy to digest.

The carbohydrate of milk is in the form of the sugar *lactose*, also called *milk sugar*. Milk sugar is only very slightly sweet, which is fortunate because we soon tire of sweet foods. As it is, the flavour of milk is very mild so that we do not tire of it, and it can be used in the preparation of many cooked dishes without giving them a 'milk flavour'.

Milk contains bacteria and easily 'sours' when it is stored. This is because enzymes in the bacteria convert milk sugar into a sour-tasting acid called *lactic acid*. This acid coagulates the casein in milk and turns it into a solid called *curds*. Now you will understand why it is important to have fresh milk supplies daily, and why milk must be stored carefully (see page 179)

★★★ **Keypoint.**

$$\text{Fresh milk} \xrightarrow{\text{on standing}} \text{Sour milk}$$

$$\text{Lactose} \xrightarrow[\text{bacteria}]{\text{enzymes in}} \text{Lactic acid}$$

Milk *curdles* more rapidly when it is warm than when it is cold, and so only fresh milk should be kept hot. For example, if you want to prepare a vacuum flask of hot coffee for a picnic, use fresh milk. If you do not, you may find that when you open the flask you have an unpleasant curdled mass! The presence of acid hastens curdling, and so you need to take care when preparing such dishes as tomato soup, because the acidity of the tomato juice may be enough to curdle the hot milk.

★★ **Activity.** Divide a little cold milk into two portions. To one add a little (e.g. a tablespoon) vinegar and to the other lemon juice. Repeat using hot milk instead of cold. Observe what happens and try to explain it. (Vinegar and lemon juice are both acids, i.e. sour.)

★ **?** If you wanted to make coffee with milk that was possibly a little sour, would it be better to serve the coffee iced or hot?

★ **?** Stewed rhubarb is very acid. What may happen when you add to it hot custard or milk?

The amount of fat and milk sugar in milk is small. Yet although milk does not have a high energy value, you can see from Fig. 31

that it makes a useful contribution to our energy intake. If a child aged two to five consumed two pints of milk a day, this would supply *half* her energy needs.

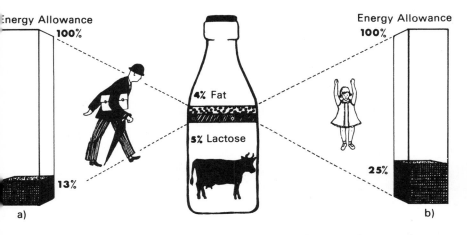

Fig. 31. One pint of milk daily contributes (a) 13% of the energy allowance of a fairly active man and (b) 25% of the energy allowance of a two- to five-year-old girl or boy

Vitamins and minerals in milk. Milk is a valuable source of several vitamins. The oil droplets contain vitamins A and D, while the watery part of the milk is rich in vitamin B_2 and also contains useful amounts of vitamins B_1 and C. Unfortunately some of these vitamins may be destroyed before the milk reaches us if it is not carefully treated. For example, if you leave your milk on the doorstep in the sun for several hours, you will destroy most of the vitamins B_2 and C. Also if you heat milk for any length of time you will destroy some of the vitamins B_1 and C.

We have already noted that milk is a good source of calcium and phosphorus. Unfortunately it is a poor source of iron. Cows' milk contains less iron than human milk and so, for example, when young babies are bottle-fed iron-rich foods should be added to the diet.

★ ? Why is milk best stored in a cool place away from direct sunlight?

Treatment of milk

Milk is such a rich source of nutrients that it is an ideal place for the growth of bacteria. Although milk should be nearly free of bacteria at the time it is obtained from a clean healthy cow, it is impossible to keep it in this condition. Bacteria from the person who milks the cow (or the milking machine), from the milk churn and from the air pass into the milk, where they settle down happily to grow and multiply! Most of these bacteria are harmless and do nothing more than turn the milk sour. Bacteria from unhealthy cows, however, may well be harmful and cause tuberculosis. In the past thousands of people and cattle have died each year in Great Britain alone from this cause.

Milk is such an important food that we must make sure that a supply of clean, fresh milk is available for everyone. We are very lucky in Britain to-day that this is so and that milk arrives on our doorsteps as regularly as the newspaper. We can make sure that milk is safe by means of heat treatment and by creating herds of cows in which harmful bacteria are absent.

★★★ **Keypoint.** The most common forms of heat treatment are pasteurization and sterilization.

Milk is pasteurized by heating to at least 72°C for at least 15 seconds and then rapidly cooling it. Sterilized milk is given a much more severe heat treatment. It is first *homogenized* by heating to 65°C and forcing it through a small hole. This breaks up the oil droplets into very small particles, and reduces the tendency of the fat in the milk to form a separate cream layer during storage. The milk is then placed in bottles which are sealed with metal caps before heating at 100–110°C for 30–40 minutes. Sterilized milk will keep for at least a week and usually much longer.

Pasteurization of milk kills most bacteria present and is of great benefit in giving us safe milk. It also destroys small amounts of vitamins B_1 and C, but this loss is of very little importance compared to the benefit of having clean wholesome milk always available.

The flavour of pasteurized milk is so similar to that of untreated milk that it is almost impossible to tell the difference between them. The one disadvantage of pasteurized milk is that it does not keep long. Sterilized milk, however, keeps longer because it has been given a more severe heat treatment. It has a different flavour from fresh milk, and for this reason many people do not like it. New processes, however, can produce sterilized milk—known as ultra-high temperature milk (U.H.T.)—that will keep for months and that tastes similar to pasteurized milk. Sterilization produces a bigger loss of vitamins than pasteurization but this loss is not important. There is probably a big future for U.H.T. milk because it can be bought in supermarkets and kept for months in sealed cartons without refrigeration.

TYPES OF FRESH MILK ON SALE IN GREAT BRITAIN

Type	Nature
Farm	Bottled on the farm; not heat-treated; is best avoided especially by children
Pasteurized	Heat-treated to kill most bacteria; taste little affected; some vitamin B_1 and C destroyed
Homogenized pasteurized	Differs from pasteurized in that it is homogenized to disperse the fat; does not form a cream layer
Sterilized	Homogenized milk heated to a higher temperature than pasteurized; has a 'cooked' taste; much vitamin B_1 and C destroyed; proteins coagulated. Keeps well
Ultra-high temperature (U.H.T.) milk	Homogenized milk heated to a high temperature (135–150°C) for 1–3 seconds; resembles pasteurized milk in flavour and food value; sold in sealed cartons and will keep for several months without refrigeration

★★★ **Keypoint.** All milk sold in Britain is T.T. tested, i.e. it comes from cows that are *Tuberculin Tested* (free from tuberculosis bacteria).

★★ **Activity.** Find out as much as you can about the types and grades (e.g. Channel Island milk which costs more) available in your district. How can these be identified by the colour of the milk-bottle top?

You will remember that milk is nearly nine-tenths water, and it is therefore a very bulky food and so expensive to transport. Some of this water may be removed by evaporation to produce *evaporated milk* or, if sugar is added, *sweetened condensed milk*. The evaporation is carried out at a low temperature (below 70°C) to avoid giving the milk a cooked flavour and to prevent coagulation of proteins. Such milk is sealed in cans and keeps until the can is opened.

Evaporated milk contains about 25% less water than fresh milk, but it is still a rather watery food. Most of the water in milk is removed in the production of *dried milk*, which is a powder. Dried milk is very rich in nutrients and by looking at Fig. 29, you can see, for example, that 23 g of dried milk contains as much calcium as 300 g of fresh milk.

The conversion of fresh liquid milk into a powder enables milk to be kept for considerable periods in the most concentrated form possible. Liquid milk may also be converted into other solid foods that have good keeping qualities. The most important are butter, discussed in the last chapter, and cheese.

Cheese

How many types of cheese do you know? You will easily be able to think of about ten—or perhaps even twenty—but you will still be a long way from the total, which is the surprisingly large number of four hundred. In Great Britain alone many different varieties of cheese are made.

British cheeses vary from very soft home-made cream cheeses to hard cheeses such as Cheddar; from white-coloured Stilton to pink Cheshire; from mild-flavoured Caerphilly to strong blue Stilton. Cheese can be eaten with many different foods—raw or cooked—to form tasty and nutritious dishes. Cheese cooked with cauliflower, cheese and biscuits with celery, cheese and pineapple, cheese and macaroni are only a few examples. In Yorkshire cheese is eaten with cake and apple pie; hence the Yorkshire saying 'An apple pie wi' owt th' cheese is like a kiss wi' owt a squeeze!'

Most cheeses are made from cow's milk though a few are not;

Some well-known cheeses

★★ **Activity.** See if you can identify the following cheeses in the picture above; Cheddar, Double Gloucester, Camembert, Blue Stilton, Edam (the rich, round, red one from Holland), Brie (the very flat one from France) and Gruyère (the one with the holes from Switzerland). The 'black one' is called *Tome de raisin*; it is a processed cheese from France covered with grape seeds!

for example, from Norway comes a chocolate-coloured goat's milk cheese and from France comes Roquefort cheese made from sheep's milk. The details of cheese making vary for different cheeses, but the main features are similar, and we can use Cheddar cheese as an example (see page 86).

Cheese is a most nutritious food as you would expect from the fact that a pint of milk produces only about 60 grammes of cheese. You can see just what a rich source of nutrients cheese is if you look at Fig. 32. Cheese does not contain carbohydrate because the lactose in milk is converted into lactic acid during manufacture, but it contains every other class of nutrient. It is an excellent source of protein and calcium and also of fat and vitamin A.

83

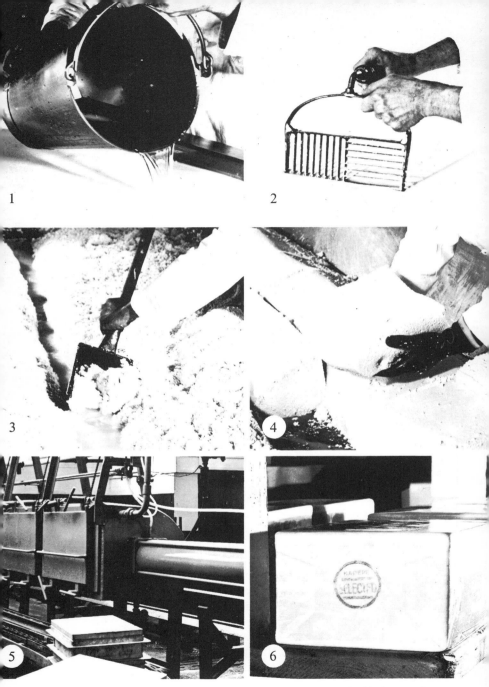

Making cheddar cheese. Milk is pasteurized and (1) a 'starter' added to turn it sour; it is warmed and rennet added. (2) The milk clots into solid curd which is cut into pieces and (3) the liquid remaining is drained off. (4) The curd is turned and cut into small pieces; (5) pressed in moulds and (6) stored until mature

Cheese is a concentrated food, 60 g being produced from a pint of milk

★ ? When cheese is made from milk what nutrients are lost? Milk contains carbohydrate in the form of lactose but cheese does not. How do you explain this? What causes liquid milk to turn into solid cheese?

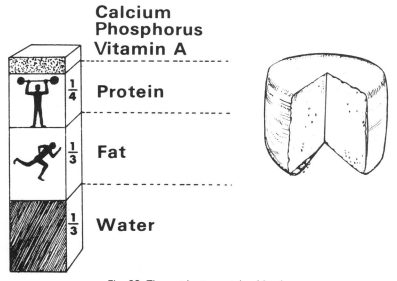

Calcium
Phosphorus
Vitamin A

$\frac{1}{4}$ **Protein**

$\frac{1}{3}$ **Fat**

$\frac{1}{3}$ **Water**

Fig. 32. The nutrients contained in cheese

Cheese is a rich source of proteins of high biological value. It is a highly concentrated food and so we only eat a little at a time. It is especially useful for packed meals and camping, when foods of small bulk are needed. It is more difficult to digest than milk and should be chewed well. Cooking does not improve its digestibility, and over-cooking makes it more difficult to digest because of over-coagulation of protein. Because cheese is so rich in protein and fat it is best eaten with a carbohydrate-rich food, such as bread or macaroni.

★★★ **Keypoint.** Cheese has a high food value, being rich in protein, calcium and fat. The cheaper cheeses (e.g. Cheddar and Cheshire) are good sources of protein of high biological value and are excellent value for money.

Eggs

Nowadays we think of an egg simply as food, but in the past it has been important in magic, witchcraft and fortune-telling among other things. For instance if you wanted to know your fortune in marriage, you let three drops of egg white fall from the point of an egg into water—on New Year's Eve! From the shape of the egg white in the water you could work out your marriage hopes with certainty! To-day we no longer have such faith in the powers of the egg, though we still have our chocolate eggs as a symbol of 'new birth' at Eastertime.

Even if we no longer believe in the magic powers of eggs, they still remain a valuable food. When we talk of eggs in connection with food, we nearly always mean hens' eggs, and so these are the sort we shall describe here.

A hen's egg has three parts; shell, white and yolk (Fig. 33). The shell is hard, being mainly calcium carbonate (chalk), and it protects the contents of the egg from harm. The colour of the shell varies from white to brown, and some people still believe that the colour has something to do with the quality of the egg. This is nonsense, however, as the colour depends on the breed of hen. In general heavy hens, such as Rhode Island Reds, lay brown eggs while lighter hens, such as Leghorns, lay white ones.

The hard shell contains tiny holes which allow gases to pass through; it is said to be *porous*. A fresh egg contains a small air pocket but as it gets older air passes into it and the air pocket gets

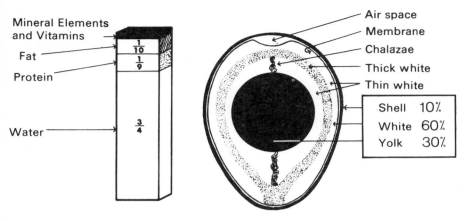

Fig. 33. The structure of a hen's egg and its nutrient content (excluding shell)

bigger. Unfortunately bacteria pass into the egg with the air, and so eggs are liable to go bad on storage. The well-known 'bad egg smell' of rotten eggs, due to hydrogen sulphide gas, is caused by action of bacteria on the sulphur in the egg protein. When eggs are stored they should be put into a cool dry place with the blunt end (which contains the air pocket) at the top. Because their shells are porous eggs absorb odours from other foods and so should be stored well away from anything with a strong smell.

Eggs may be preserved by sealing the tiny holes in the shell. This may be done by putting fresh eggs into water glass solution. Water glass deposits in the holes, sealing the shell so preventing the entry of air and bacteria into the egg.

★★ **Activity.** You can test the freshness of an egg as follows: Make up a 10% salt solution and put it in a tall jar or jug. Place an egg in the salt solution and observe what happens.

Explanation. As mentioned above as an egg ages the air pocket becomes larger and hence the egg becomes lighter. Thus the older the egg, the more buoyant it is, and the nearer the surface it will float. Repeat the experiment with one egg that is known to be fresh and one that is known to be old.

Inside the shell is a thin membrane separating the shell and air pocket from the white. Egg white is a colourless liquid being about seven-eighths water and one-eighth protein. The main protein is *ovalbumin*. In a fresh egg, the white surrounds a central yolk and is divided into regions of thick and thin white. Egg quality is now defined by EEC regulations (Fig. 34).

Class A (First quality)

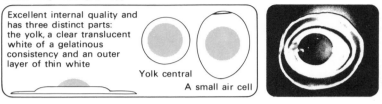

Excellent internal quality and has three distinct parts: the yolk, a clear translucent white of a gelatinous consistency and an outer layer of thin white

Yolk central

A small air cell

Class B (Second quality)

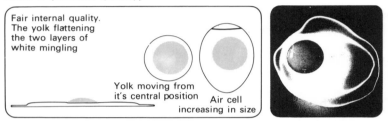

Fair internal quality. The yolk flattening the two layers of white mingling

Yolk moving from it's central position

Air cell increasing in size

Class C (Third quality)

Suitable for the manufacture of foodstuffs for human consumption, but which are not on sale in shops

Fig. 34. Egg quality as defined by EEC regulations

The yolk of an egg is suspended in the white—being held in position by the *chalazae*—and is a rich source of nutrients. It is about one-half water, one-third fat and one-quarter protein. The fat, like that of milk, is emulsified in water and so is easy to digest. The colour of the yolk varies from light yellow to deep orange, and though you may prefer the deeper colour, do not make the mistake of thinking it is necessarily more nutritious than the lighter coloured yolk. Colour depends upon the diet of the hen.

★★★ **Keypoint.** A hen's egg has high nutritional value, as you might expect from the fact that it is designed as a complete food supply for an unborn chick growing inside it.

Although it is not a complete food for humans it contains a good supply of body-building nutrients; protein of very high biological

88

value, and small amounts of calcium, phosphorus and sulphur. It is unfortunate that most of the mineral element content of an egg is in the shell which we cannot eat.

Eggs are not rich energy foods, but they do contain some fat in an easily digestible form. They also supply useful amounts of protective nutrients, especially iron and vitamins A and D; also some B vitamins.

★★★ **Keypoint.** *Candling. The quality of eggs is tested by candling* in which the interior of the egg is made visible by an intense light.

In recent years great changes have taken place in egg production. Free-range hens are now relatively rare and most hens are reared on a factory scale in huge hen-houses. This has led to chickens becoming one of the cheapest flesh foods available and eggs remain a fairly cheap way of buying animal protein.

Eggs are invaluable in cooking as you will see in Chapter 11.

Meat

Roast meat is still the basis of the traditional Sunday dinner in many homes in Great Britain. It is a good nutritional choice for the main item in the meal, because it is not only a fine protein food, but also a useful source of vitamins, mineral elements and energy.

When we talk about meat we usually mean lean meat, that is the flesh (muscular parts) of animals such as the bullock, pig and sheep which supply us with beef, pork and mutton respectively. We also eat the flesh of poultry, such as chicken and turkey, and of wild or 'game' birds, such as partridge and pheasant.

Muscle tissue is made up of tiny thread-like fibres which are held together by connective tissue to form bundles. Such tissue is about three-quarters water, one-quarter protein together with small amounts of fat, mineral elements and vitamins. The tenderness of lean flesh depends upon the nature of the muscle fibres and the amount of connective tissue. In old animals and in animals which have been very active there is a large amount of connective tissue, and this is tough and difficult to digest; also the muscle fibres are thick and tough. Therefore such meat must be carefully cooked if it is to become tender (see Chapter 11).

★★ **Activity.** The prices of different cuts of meat vary greatly according to quality even though the nutritional value varies little. Visit a butcher's shop and try to identify the following cuts and find out their relative cost.

Cuts of beef: neck, middle rib, brisket, sirloin, rump, topside, silverside and leg. These can be identified from the diagram overleaf.

Which is the best value for money in terms of their protein content and what special precautions might be needed in cooking it?

Meat is not cooked and eaten until it has been stored—or hung as it is called—for a time. This is because meat from freshly killed animals is tough, whereas after it has been hung it is more tender and has more flavour. The time for which meat is hung varies, but in the case of 'game' birds it is continued until the meat is 'high'; that is until it has started to decompose due to attack by micro-organisms.

★★★ **Keypoint.** Meat is mainly important as a body-building food, and it contains proteins of high biological value. In muscle fibres the proteins *myosin* (the main protein of meat) and *actin* are responsible for muscle contraction.

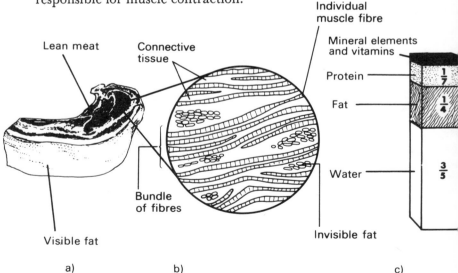

Fig. 35. (a) A rib of lean beef showing (b) a magnified portion of the muscle tissue (c) The average nutrient content of beef

Meat contains useful amounts of phosphorus but little calcium. The small amount of fat in lean meat is called 'invisible fat', because it is present in such minute particles in connective tissue that it cannot be seen. When you buy meat from the butchers you usually get some fat along with the lean. The amount of this visible fat, which is found just under the animal's skin, is much larger than the amount of invisible fat and explains why meat as eaten is a useful energy food. Meat also contains B vitamins and iron.

The organs of animals—such as liver and kidney—are also eaten, and these are called *offal*. Most offal has a higher nutritional value than flesh. Liver, for example, is one of the richest sources of iron and contains valuable amounts of vitamin A in addition to the B vitamins.

★ ? Why are some cuts of meat more tender than others and why is meat hung before it is cooked?

Main cuts from a side of English Beef (see Activity on previous page)

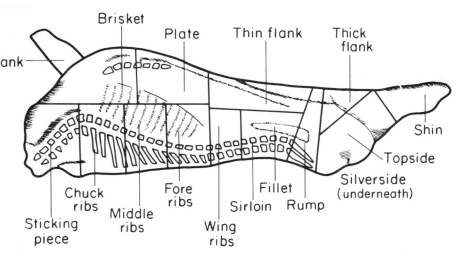

Fish

Fish is often eaten as an alternative to meat and, like meat, it is a good source of protein in the diet. Fish may be classified in various ways as follows:

Sea or fresh water fish
Scaly or smooth skinned fish
White or fat fish.

It is usually most helpful to classify fish as either white fish or fat fish. White fish have most of their fat stored in the liver and this can be extracted for use as a food supplement. Well known examples are halibut-liver oil and cod-liver oil which are valuable sources of vitamins A and D. The fat of fat fish, on the other hand, is not concentrated in one organ but is dispersed throughout the flesh, so giving it a darker colour. Oily fish such as sardines release much of this oil when cooked or canned.

Other categories of fish are shell fish such as prawns and shrimps and crustaceans such as crabs and lobsters.

★★★ **Keypoint.** Fish are mainly prized as fine body-building food. They contain roughly the same amount of protein as meat, that is about one-sixth to one-seventh of their total weight. Fish protein, like that of meat, is of high biological value.

Fish are also good suppliers of phosphorus, though not of calcium unless the bones are eaten, as is the case with tinned sardines and tinned salmon.

White fish contain very little fat and are poor energy foods. Fat fish on the other hand contain more fat and are good energy foods.

Fish supply some mineral elements and sea fish in particular are a valuable source of iodine. Fish, with the notable exception of sardines, contain very little iron. Fish contain small amounts of the B vitamins and fat fish are valuable sources of vitamins A and D.

Most fish contain much waste matter so we are unable to eat parts such as the head, tail and fins. The flesh of fish is more digestible than that of meat because it has less tough connective tissue and the muscle fibres are shorter and less tough. All the fat in fat fish is dispersed in the flesh; i.e., it is 'invisible fat'.

You can see from what we have said that white fish is just as valuable a food as meat, and that fat fish has a higher food value

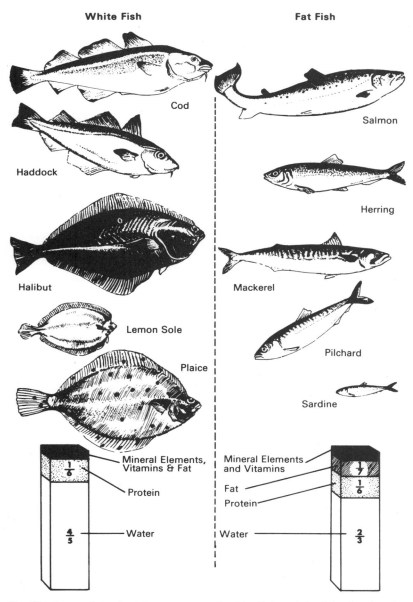

Fig. 36. Some of the best known types of white fish and fat fish showing the difference in their nutrient content

than meat. Many people seem to think that meat is the better food, but this is not true and we would do well to value fish more highly than we do. Fat fish, such as herring, have the double merit of being both cheap and nutritious. Also, fish need less cooking than meat and are more easily digested.

★★ **Activity.** Visit a fishmongers, identify as many of the fish shown in Fig. 36 as you can and list them with their relative costs under the headings, White Fish and Fat Fish. Which would be the best buy in terms of nutritional value?

The nature of the fish we eat is likely to change considerably in the future. In the past much of our fish have come from the seas around Iceland. Two of our most popular fish, cod and haddock, are found in this area. Now that British trawlers are not allowed to fish in Icelandic seas, we will be more dependent on fish caught in the seas around Britain. Supplies of plaice, haddock, herring and mackerel are still likely to be plentiful but cod will be much scarcer.

Already saithe—or coley as it is better known—is being used to replace cod in some fish fingers. In Britain we are very conservative about trying new varieties of fish. For example, blue ling which is found in the seas around Britain and popular in France, is hardly known in the U.K. Whatever varieties of fish we eat in the future, however, a large proportion will be in convenience form, particularly as quick frozen fish. Consumption of frozen fish is steadily increasing and accounts for more than a quarter of all fish eaten.

New protein foods

New sources of protein. In many parts of the world protein food is in short supply and even in Western countries animal protein foods have become very expensive. In searching for new sources of food we shall, therefore, be especially on the lookout for new sources of cheap protein. We obtain much of our protein food indirectly by growing plants, which are mainly carbohydrate, and feeding the plants to animals. Eventually we eat the animals which supply us with valuable animal protein. Unfortunately this is not a profitable method of producing protein because we get back less than one tenth of the protein that we fed to the animal!

Soya beans (*top*) contain protein of high biological value. Soya bean flour can be spun into fibres (*bottom photograph*) which have the chewy texture of meat fibres

It would clearly be much simpler and more profitable if we could extract the protein from the plants directly without getting an animal to do this for us. Many plant materials, such as grass, cannot be eaten by us directly, because they are mostly cellulose and so indigestible. However, we can extract the protein from such plants. At present we waste many millions of tons of plant material every year, so that in the future we may obtain large amounts of concentrated protein food from such sources.

Although the quality of protein in most vegetable material is low, that of soya beans is an exception. Soya beans, and soya bean flour, have been a valuable source of high quality protein in the diets of Japan and China for many centuries, and they are now being grown increasingly in other countries, particularly in the United States. Although soya beans are grown mainly as a source of vegetable oil, new methods of processing them have been developed in the United States.

★★★ **Keypoint.** The use of soya beans and products containing them should be encouraged. They grow easily in warm countries and have a high food value. They contain up to 40% protein of high biological value, and about 18% fat together with some B vitamins.

One of the greatest problems of new protein sources is the difficulty of getting them accepted by the people who would benefit from eating them. In order to try to overcome such difficulties soya-bean flour has been used to make products resembling meat.

One of the best known of these is texturised vegetable protein, TVP. This is made by passing a mixture of defatted soya flour, additives and water through an extruder at a high temperature and pressure. The result is a dried product containing about 8% moisture that has a chewy texture. TVP is available in many shapes and sizes, including chunks, flakes and granules, in both unflavoured and flavoured forms. Another product made by spinning protein extracted from soya beans has a more meat-like texture than the texturised product but has the disadvantage that it is more expensive. Most soya bean products are produced in dried form and so are easy to store.

Vegetable protein can be used on its own but more usually it is added to a meat product as a ' meat extender ' so as to give it a high protein content at minimum cost. Vegetable proteins are

96

regularly used in schools, hospitals and canteens to replace part of the meat in traditional dishes though in Britain it is recommended that not more than 10% of meat should be replaced in this way. An increasing range of products—such as minces, stews, curries, burgers and burger-style dried mixes—containing vegetable protein are now available.

★★★ **Keypoint.** It makes better sense to grow soya beans as a food for man rather than crops to feed to animals. Whereas one acre used for raising beef will provide enough protein for one person for **77 days** the same area used to grow soya beans would provide enough protein for **2,000 days.**

We can also hope to obtain protein from non-plant protein materials which at present are wasted. When vegetable oils are extracted from groundnuts, coconuts and the like, a valuable but indigestible protein-rich residue remains. This is often used as cattle food or fertilizer, but if processed to remove the indigestible part it could be converted into a valuable protein food. In a similar way we can produce a highly nutritious protein-rich flour from whole fish.

Finally, some micro-organisms such as yeast and fungi are able to grow, multiply and build up protein very quickly starting from sugar and various mineral elements. In the future cultivation of yeasts and fungi should be able to supply us with useful amounts of good quality protein. Recently waste material produced during oil refining has been used as a source of nutrients. Several major oil companies are spending many millions of pounds developing this idea.

Perhaps one day we shall grow yeast instead of rearing cattle, for whereas half a ton of bullock only produces one pound of protein in 24 hours, half a ton of yeast can produce *fifty* tons of protein in the same time!

It is to be hoped that in the future these new sources of protein will help overcome the lack of protein at present prevalent in many parts of the world.

★ ? Meat protein is in short supply. What new sources of high-quality protein may become available in the future?

6 Vitamins, Mineral Elements and Water

We have already seen that we need fats and carbohydrates to supply us with energy and proteins for body-building. In addition to these nutrients, however, you will remember that our bodies require vitamins, mineral elements and water. Vitamins and mineral elements are needed for regulating the many chemical processes which go on inside our bodies. They help to protect us against ill-health and disease and so they are sometimes called *protective* nutrients, though this is rather a vague term which is best avoided. Mineral elements are also important for body-building processes of course, as we have seen in the last chapter. Last but not least there is water. Our bodies are almost two-thirds water, and since we lose several pints of it every day in various ways it is obvious that a regular supply of it is essential.

VITAMIN MAGIC

What are vitamins? Most people find this a hard question to answer, because to-day, more than half a century after their discovery, they still seem to have something of magic and mystery about them. Can you ever remember having handled, tasted or seen a vitamin? You can probably talk about carbohydrates with some confidence because you have seen and tasted sugar which is pure carbohydrate and you are familiar with cereal foods that are mainly carbohydrate. But when it comes to vitamins we only know that food contains them in tiny quantities and we cannot imagine what they are like.

If we accept the importance of vitamins and the fact that they are essential in our diet we are still left with the basic question— what are they? Perhaps we should start by saying what they are not. They are not like the major ingredients of food—fats, carbohydrates and proteins—which each form a compact and readily identifiable group. For example, fats all have a number of characteristics in common; they have a greasy feel, they will not dissolve in water and so on and we recognize them when we see them or eat them. Not only do they look alike but they all have a similar function in our bodies—they provide us with energy. Moreover we eat quite large amounts of fat and also of protein and carbohydrate. When we turn to the vitamins, which are most simply identified by letters A, B, C and so on, we find that each vitamin is different from the others so that they do not form a compact group like the other nutrients. Some are liquids, some are solids, some dissolve in water, some dissolve in fat. In addition they each have their own specific job to do in the body and this is quite distinct and different from that of the other vitamins. In view of all these differences between vitamins it is not surprising that people find it hard to visualize them, nor that they find it hard to understand their significance.

★★★ **Keypoint.** Vitamins have little in common and really the only common factor that causes them to be grouped together is the fact that they are all essential to the body's well-being and that they are all required in tiny amounts.

One way to take the mystery out of vitamins is to handle and see them. For example, you can buy vitamin C tablets at the chemists and you will remember (page 27) that they are made of a white solid which has a sour taste typical of an acid. Such tablets are made from synthetic vitamin C made entirely in the laboratory but it is important to realize that the synthetic vitamin is the same as the natural vitamin extracted from fruit. There are some people who claim that the vitamins contained in natural products are in some strange way different from, and superior to, vitamins made in the laboratory. This is simply not true however, although it is possible that the natural product may contain additional substances of nutritional value not present in the synthetic vitamin, which is a single substance.

The amount of vitamins contained in food is very small. For example, lemons contain only about one part of vitamin C in two thousand parts of lemon. Although this may appear to be a tiny amount, nevertheless a lemon contains about a day's supply of the vitamin for an adult. Vitamins are distributed among many

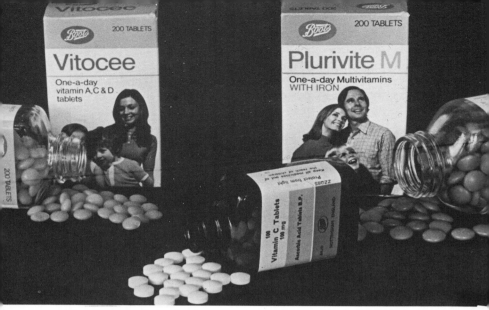

There is no magic in vitamins; you can see them and taste them when they are in tablet form as shown here

different types of food, and to ensure that all the vitamins are present in our diet in sufficient quantities for our needs, a wide variety of different foods needs to be eaten. The vitamin content of a food can vary quite considerably. This is especially so with fruit and vegetables where the vitamin content depends, amongst other things, on freshness, variety and ripeness.

Vitamins are found in small amounts in many foods. Their presence in the diet is essential because, with a few exceptions, we are unable to make them for ourselves. Vitamins are necessary for growth, and if children do not get enough of them their growth may be slowed down. When a vitamin is missing from the diet, or is in very short supply, a disease known as a *deficiency disease* may occur. Deficiency diseases have been the cause of death and much suffering for many centuries, but they can now be prevented and cured by making sure that the diet contains sufficient vitamins.

★★★ **Keypoint.** It is so important that we all receive enough vitamins that some foods have extra vitamins added to them. Flour, margarine and many baby foods and breakfast foods are fortified, or enriched with vitamins in this way.

100

★★ Activity. Look at a variety of packets of breakfast cereals and also at a margarine packet. What vitamins have been added?

★★★ Keypoint. The sources and functions of vitamins are summarized in the vitamin table below.

VITAMIN SUMMARY

Name	Main sources	Functions in the body and effect of shortage
Vitamin A	Green vegetables, milk, dairy products, margarine, fish liver oil	Necessary for healthy skin and teeth and also for normal growth and development. Deficiency will slow down growth and may lead to disorders of the skin, lowered resistance to infection and disturbances of vision such as night blindness
The B Vitamins: Thiamine, Riboflavin, Nicotinic Acid, Nicotinamide	Bread and flour, meat, milk, potatoes, yeast extract	Function as co-enzymes in many of the reactions involved in making use of food. Shortage causes loss of appetite, slows growth and development and impairs general health. Severe deficiency may lead to a deficiency disease such as pellagra or beriberi
Vitamin C (Ascorbic Acid)	Green vegetables, fruits, potatoes, blackcurrant syrup, rosehip syrup	Necessary for the proper formation of teeth, bones and blood vessels. Shortage causes a check in the growth of children and if prolonged may lead to the disease scurvy
Vitamin D	Margarine, butter, milk, fish liver oils, fat fish	Necessary for the formation of strong bones and teeth. A shortage may cause rickets and possibly dental decay.

A, B, C of vitamins

Vitamins are named A, B, C and so on as mentioned above, but in addition each has a scientific name, and this is given alongside the alphabet letter in the following sections.

Vitamins are present in food in such small amounts that we use very small units to describe vitamin content. The usual units used are milligrammes (mg) and microgrammes (μg).

1 gramme = 1000 milligramme = 1 000 000 microgramme

Examples. Old potatoes contain 0·05 g vitamin C per 100 g. This is more conveniently expressed as 50 mg/100 g. Fresh milk contains 0·000 02 g vitamin C per gramme. This is more conveniently expressed as 20 mg/g.

★★ **Activity.** Cod liver oil contains 0·000 217 g vitamin D per 100 g and butter contains 0·000 001 25 g vitamin D per 100 g. Express these as mg/100 g and μg/100 g. Which of these is the most convenient?

We only require very small amounts of vitamins to remain healthy. For example, a gramme of vitamin A would be sufficient to last an adult for $3\frac{1}{2}$ years! It would be quite useless to eat this quantity and then go without for $3\frac{1}{2}$ years, however, because our bodies are only able to store limited quantities of vitamin A. Regular and adequate quantities of vitamins are required and this is especially so for the water-soluble vitamins, such as vitamin C and the B vitamins. Our bodies are unable to build up a reserve of these, and any excess over immediate requirements is excreted in the urine.

You may be surprised that such small quantities of vitamins are so important that our bodies are unable to carry on without them. In some ways vitamins are to our bodies what lubricating oil is to a machine. Only small amounts of oil are required by a machine but these small amounts are necessary if it is to run smoothly. Without oil the machine will carry on for a while, but it will run less and less smoothly and become less and less efficient. In time the machine will be unable to continue without oil and it will stop. The action of vitamins in our bodies is much like this. If our food contains less vitamins than we need we can still carry on, but our bodies are not able to make the most efficient use of our food, and

102

in time the shortage will show itself as a deficiency disease. In extreme cases of vitamin deficiency death may result.

The more important vitamins are discussed below. Several others are known but they are widely distributed in foods and there is no danger of a shortage of them.

★ ? Why do we need vitamins in small amounts regularly rather than in larger amounts once in a while?

★ ? What happens if we go short of vitamins (a) for a little while and (b) for a long while, e.g. several months?

★★ **Activity.** Go to a chemist's shop and find as many vitamins as you can. Make a list of them and describe what each looks like (ignore preparations containing more than one vitamin).

Vitamin A or Retinol. Vitamin A is a pale-yellow solid which dissolves easily in fats and oils, but not in water.

The most important sources of vitamin A in the diet are green vegetables and dairy products. Green vegetables do not contain vitamin A as such, however. They contain substances known as *carotenes*, which are easily converted by our bodies—and also by animals such as sheep and cows—into vitamin A. Carotenes are brightly coloured, and are responsible for the colour of carrots, the yellow colour of unripe tomatoes and butter and the creamy colour of cream. When vegetables are eaten our bodies are unable to convert all the carotenes to vitamin A. For this reason animal sources of the vitamin are much more effective in the diet than vegetable sources.

The vitamin A content of dairy products such as milk, butter and cheese depends upon the amount of carotenes in the food eaten by the cow. For this reason milk may be richer in vitamin A during the summer—when cows are able to feed on fresh grass—than in winter when only hay and animal feeding-stuffs are available. Vitamin A is added to many proprietary cattle foods, however, and in this case as much of the vitamin may be present in winter milk as in summer milk.

As butter and cheese are made from milk, the vitamin A from milk is present in these foods. At one time margarine contained little or no vitamin A, but nowadays margarine manufacturers must add vitamin A to it. Margarine now contains at least as much vitamin A as is present in butter.

Other good sources of vitamin A are eggs and liver. Fish liver oils are particularly rich in the vitamin and may be used to supplement the dietary sources.

Vitamin A is necessary for growth and so it is very important that babies and young children receive enough of it. Shortage in infancy during the formation of teeth may produce poor teeth, and even after the teeth have been formed lack of vitamin A may affect the enamel. A condition known as *night-blindness* may arise as a result of vitamin A shortage. Sufferers from this find it difficult to see in poor light. A severe deficiency of vitamin A may cause an eye disease which may ultimately lead to blindness. Dryness of the skin and a lower resistance to infection are also caused by a shortage of vitamin A.

The B group of vitamins. Several vitamins which have similar jobs to do in the body, and which are often found in the same foods, are included in the B group of vitamins. The B vitamins form a part of several enzyme systems in the body and they help to release the energy from food. They are, in fact, *co-enzymes*, that is substances which assist enzymes to carry out their work. The B vitamins dissolve in water, and if more is eaten than the body requires it is excreted in the urine. The more important members of the B group of vitamins are *thiamine* (which is also called vitamin B_1), *riboflavin* (also called vitamin B_2) and *nicotinamide*.

The co-enzymes which our bodies make from the B vitamins are used in releasing the energy from the carbohydrates in our food. Because the amount of carbohydrate eaten varies from person to person it is difficult to say with certainty how much B vitamins we need. A very small quantity is enough, however, and even someone with a huge appetite would only need one-fiftieth of a gramme each day.

Vitamin B_1 or Thiamine. Thiamine is a white water-soluble solid. It is made artificially on quite a large scale for adding to white flour to replace the thiamine which is lost during milling. Thiamine is found in many foodstuffs. The main sources in a normal diet are bread, potatoes, meat and milk. Because it dissolves easily in water, as much as half the thiamine present in vegetables may be lost when they are boiled.

Deficiency of thiamine produces a check in the growth of children together with a loss of appetite and fatigue. Severe shortage can cause the disease *beriberi*.

104

Beriberi is almost unknown in this country, but it causes much suffering in Far Eastern countries where the standard of living is very low. In these countries the main article of diet is polished rice which contains little or no thiamine. Polished rice is made by removing from rice the husk and an outer layer or membrane called the silverskin. Both husk and silverskin contain appreciable quantities of thiamine. They are removed to improve the appearance of the rice—and because the husk is hard and difficult to digest.

You may think it strange that people should suffer as a result of the deliberate removal of a nutrient from a food. It is, indeed, unfortunate that this should be so. A similar situation exists in Western countries where most of the thiamine present in wheat is lost in the production of white flour. To counteract this, thiamine is added to all flour except wholemeal flour, and it provides about one-fifth of all the thiamine in an average diet.

Vitamin B₂ or riboflavin. Riboflavin is a yellow crystalline substance which is found in many plant and animal tissues. It is only slightly soluble in water, and so not much is lost when food is boiled. It is, however, sensitive to light and three-quarters of the riboflavin in milk may be destroyed when milk is allowed to stand in direct sunlight for three hours. This is a good reason for not leaving milk on the doorstep any longer than is absolutely necessary! Riboflavin is found in quite a large number of foods. Milk, meat, potatoes, cereals and eggs are the main sources in the average diet.

A shortage of riboflavin causes a check in the growth of children, and in addition sores may develop.

Nicotinic acid and nicotinamide. Nicotinic acid and nicotinamide are both white crystalline solids. Nicotinic acid was first made—long before it was known to be a vitamin—from nicotine which is present in tobacco. In food, however, it is not obtained from nicotine nor is it formed during tobacco smoking. Nicotinic acid is called *niacin* in the United States because it was feared that some people would assume that nicotine absorbed during smoking could serve as a source of the vitamin. Large quantities of nicotinic acid are now made for addition to white flour to replace that lost during milling.

Nicotinic acid was first found in food about fifty years ago, when it was discovered in rice polishings. Plants contain the vitamin as nicotinic acid and animal tissues contain it as nicotinamide. Both substances are similar and equally active as vitamins, because nicotinic acid is converted into nicotinamide by our bodies when we eat it. Meat, bread and potatoes are the main sources of them both in the diet.

A deficiency of nicotinic acid causes a check in the growth of children and, if severe, the disease *pellagra*.

SUMMARY TABLE OF OTHER B VITAMINS

Name	Main sources	Function
Pyridoxine (Vitamin B_6)	Meat, fish, eggs, whole cereals, some vegetables	Metabolism of amino acids and formation of haemoglobin
Cobalamin (Vitamin B_{12})	Animal foods especially liver and kidneys, fatty fish, eggs	Cobalamin, folic acid and iron required for formation of red blood cells. Deficiency produces anaemia.
Folic acid	Many foods especially liver; also kidney, green vegetables, bran	
Pantothenic acid	Many foods especially animal foods, cereals and legumes	Aids release of energy from fat and carbohydrate
Biotin	Liver, kidney, egg yolk, milk, bananas	Essential for metabolism of fat

★ ? The B vitamins are said to act as coenzymes in the body. What does this mean?

Vitamin C or ascorbic acid. This is a white, sharp-tasting solid which dissolves easily in water. It occurs mainly in fruits and vegetables. Blackcurrants and strawberries are particularly rich in the vitamin but unfortunately many popular eating apples, pears and plums contain only small amounts. Green vegetables, potatoes and fresh fruit supply most of the vitamin C in our diet.

The amount of vitamin C present in vegetables is greatest in the periods of active growth in spring and early summer. Storage

106

decreases the ascorbic acid content and old potatoes contain much less than new potatoes. Potatoes are a very valuable source of vitamin C, although weight for weight they contain less of the vitamin than green vegetables. A normal serving of boiled new potatoes provides about 90% of the recommended daily intake of vitamin C.

As much as 75% of the vitamin C contained in green vegetables may be lost when they are cooked. This loss can be avoided by eating green vegetables raw in salads, but the amount which can be eaten in this way is small. Even allowing for losses in cooking, larger quantities of vitamin C are obtained from a normal serving of cabbage than from a normal serving of lettuce. Five times as much vitamin C is obtainable from 100 g of cooked cabbage as from 25 g—which is about as much as one normally eats—of raw lettuce. Enough vitamin C to last a whole day is contained in 25 g of raw cabbage, which is a much better source of the vitamin than lettuce.

Cow's milk contains only about one-third as much vitamin C as human milk, and some of this is destroyed during pasteurization. Exposure of milk to sunlight also destroys some of the vitamin C. It is important that babies, and particularly those fed

★★★ **Keypoint.** Fruit and vegetables supply nearly 30% of the vitamin A and nearly 90% of the vitamin C in an average British diet.
★★ **Activity.** Identify as many fruit and vegetables as you can in the picture below. Can you see any that would be a good source of vitamin A or C?

on cow's milk which has been boiled, should be given extra vitamin C. Rose-hip syrup or concentrated orange or blackcurrant juice can be used for this purpose. When babies progress to a mixed diet there is less need for such supplements, and at two years of age the normal diet should provide sufficient vitamin C.

Foods—such as yeast, egg-yolk, meats and cereals—which are rich in B vitamins, usually contain little or no vitamin C.

Effects of vitamin C deficiency. A shortage of vitamin C in the diet prevents children growing properly. Severe deficiency may cause the disease *scurvy*, which has been known for hundreds of years and was at one time very common in Europe in the winter months when fresh food was short. It was especially troublesome to sailors who were unable to get fresh food. The cause of the disease was not known, nor any way of curing it though many strange methods were tried. One British admiral tried to cure his sailors of scurvy by burying them in boxes of earth normally used for growing vegetables for salads! At that time canned food and salted meat were the main foods eaten on board ship and fresh fruit and vegetables were not thought necessary as the following verse makes clear:

> *The scurvy flew through the schooner's crew*
> *As they sailed on an Arctic sea.*
> *They were far from land and their food was canned,*
> *So they got no vitamin C.*
> *For ' Devil's the use of orange juice ',*
> *The skipper 'ad said, said he.*
> *They were victualled with pickled pork, my dears,*
> *Those mariners bold and free,*
> *Yet life's but brief on the best corned beef*
> *If you don't get vitamin C.*
> *Journal of St Bartholomew's Hospital*

During the eighteenth century it became clear that scurvy could be prevented and cured by eating fruits and vegetables or their juices. Once this was realized lemon juice was carried by ships for use in preventing scurvy. Unfortunately, however, outbreaks of scurvy still occurred for a very long time after it was known that fruit juice would prevent it. During the Crimean War in the middle of the last century more British soldiers died from scurvy than were killed in action. This great loss of life could have been prevented, for ample supplies of fruit juice had been sent from

108

England, but it was never distributed to the troops. Happily the disease is fairly uncommon in Britain at the present time.

A shortage of vitamin C not severe enough to cause scurvy may make the mouth and gums easily infected and slow down the rate at which broken bones and wounds heal. Some people think that colds last longer if the body is not getting enough vitamin C. Indeed some people try to cure colds by taking large doses of vitamin C—usually about a gramme—each day. In spite of the large number of so-called remedies available it is still just as true as ever it was that a cold lasts seven days if you treat it and a week if you leave it alone!

Vitamin D. Vitamin D is a white solid which dissolves in oils and fats but not in water. It is not present in many foods and is found only in foods of animal origin. Fish liver oils are by far the richest source. Eggs and dairy products also contain some. Because it is found in only a few foods there is more danger of a shortage of vitamin D than of any other vitamin. For this reason synthetic vitamin D is now added to all table margarine made in this country, and also to many baby foods. Margarine contains about five times as much vitamin D as butter and it provides about one third of the vitamin D in the average diet.

Vitamin D is necessary for the proper formation of bones, and a baby or child who does not receive enough will suffer from the disease called *rickets*. At one time rickets was very common in this country, but as a result of better feeding it is now uncommon. Recently rickets in children has been increasing in some British cities, though the total number of cases remains small. Rickets can be treated by exposure to sunlight or any other source of ultra-violet light (e.g. a sun-lamp). This is because vitamin D is formed in the skin under the influence of ultra-violet light.

Vitamin D is also essential for healthy teeth. Not only does it help to form good teeth, but it also helps to prevent infection of existing teeth. It is needed by our bodies before proper use can be made of the calcium and phosphorus in our food. This explains why a shortage of vitamin D has such a bad effect on the bones and teeth.

Because vitamin D is so important for the formation of strong bones and healthy teeth it is vital that children should receive enough of it. Young children should take fish liver oil or a vitamin D concentrate regularly.

109

Sunbathing is more than a pleasant recreation because sunlight forms vitamin D in the skin. Sunlight is more important than diet as a source of vitamin D.

★ ? What diseases can you name that result from a shortage of vitamins in the diet?

Vitamins E and K. We are unlikely to go short of these two vitamins as any normal diet will supply enough. They are both fat-soluble. Vitamin E is found in eggs and vegetable oils. Vitamin K is widely distributed in foods and green vegetables and fish liver oils are good sources. It is needed for the clotting of blood.

MINERAL ELEMENTS

We have already seen in Chapter 5 that mineral elements play a most important part in building up our bodies. They are also, however, important in other ways as follows:

(1) in the control of body processes,
(2) as essential parts of every cell in the body,
(3) as soluble salts in all the fluids circulating round the body.

Mineral elements which have a controlling function are found as constituents of cells or in the body fluids. Most of them are adequately provided by a well-balanced diet, but shortage of iron and calcium may easily occur.

Sodium and chlorine. All the body fluids contain sodium and chlorine in the form of sodium chloride. Our bodies are continually losing salt in urine and perspiration. The concentration of salt in the body fluids must be maintained at a certain level, and since there is no way of controlling the loss of salt from the body, all the salt lost must be replaced. If our food did not contain enough salt to replace that lost, our bodies would soon give an alarm signal in the form of painful cramps.

The fact that salt is essential for health has been realized for thousands of years. In countries where salt is scarce it is prized and has been used as money. Salt was in short supply in this country in the past and the Roman forces of occupation were paid part of their wages in salt. Indeed this is the origin of our modern word ' salary ' which means literally salt money. As little as sixty years ago salt was used as money in Ethiopia even for paying taxes and fines!

The amount of salt lost from the body can vary considerably because some people perspire more than others. Heavy manual workers need more salt than office workers, for example, because they are likely to lose more salt in perspiration. This is true also of people who live in hot countries. In this country about 4 g of salt is needed daily by an adult following a normal occupation. Salt is present in most foods but the actual quantities obtained from food are not important. Most people get more than enough from the salt used in cooking and as a condiment. Salt is also used by our bodies for making the hydrochloric acid present in the gastric juice. An excess of salt is removed from the body by the kidneys and is excreted in the urine.

★ ? In what ways is salt lost from the body? Why do coal miners need more salt than typists?

Iron. The body of an adult contains about 4 g of iron—roughly the amount in a nail 7 cm long. It is a most important mineral element because it enables us to take the oxygen from the air and use it in the oxidation processes involved in releasing energy from

The amount of iron in an adult is roughly the same as in this nail, which is 7 cm long

ood. Iron is an essential part of the compound *haemoglobin* which makes red blood cells red. The job of the red blood cells is to carry oxygen from the lungs to the tissues where it is needed for releasing the energy from sugars. Every cell in the body must be supplied with oxygen and if the number of red cells in our blood were to fall below a certain level it would be difficult for the blood to supply the tissues with enough oxygen. People in this condition are said to be *anaemic* and they are usually given iron tablets to assist in making new red blood cells.

Haemoglobin combines with oxygen in our lungs and carries it to every part of our bodies, giving up its oxygen to the cells requiring it. Each molecule of haemoglobin can combine with one molecule of oxygen, and when it does so it becomes brighter red in colour. When it gives up the oxygen it changes back to a much duller, purplish red. The bluish veins on our wrists or on the backs of our hands contain blood that has given up its oxygen to the tissues. It is being pumped back up our arms to the lungs where it will pick up a further supply of oxygen.

Red blood cells do not last for ever but have a life of about four months. The body is very thrifty with the iron contained in the old red blood cells, however, and re-uses most of it to make new ones. Some additional iron is needed, and this is especially so when the volume of blood is increasing, that is when a child is growing. It is obviously important to have sufficient iron in our food and it is therefore most unfortunate that it is one of the mineral elements which may be lacking in an average diet. To try to prevent this, iron is now added to all flour in this country except wholemeal flour.

★★★ **Keypoint.** Bread and flour products provide about a third of the iron in an average diet, the other main suppliers being meat and vegetables.

★ ? After giving blood, donors are asked to take iron tablets for the next few days. What do you think is the reason for this?

Iodine. Iodine is another mineral element which is essential to the proper working of our bodies. The iodine in our food is transported to a small gland—called the thyroid gland—at the base of the throat. It is used to make a compound called *thyroxine*.

If enough iodine is not obtained from food or drinking-water a condition known as *goitre* may result. In this disease the thyroid

112

gland becomes enlarged and is visible as a large swelling or 'growth' at the base of the throat. Goitre is sometimes called 'Derbyshire neck' because it was at one time common in Derbyshire. Because of the swelling—which can be large and unsightly —goitre is usually regarded as a disfiguring ailment. This has not always been the case, however, and in eighteenth-century France a lady's beauty was thought to be enhanced by the possession of a small goitre!

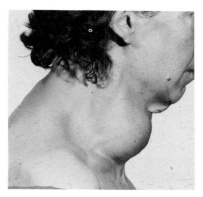

Goitre causes unsightly swelling
of the neck

Thyroxine has many jobs to do in the body, but one of its most important tasks is to control the rate at which the body burns up food and converts it into energy. When we are working hard the reactions going on inside our bodies must be speeded up to provide us with enough energy. Even when we are resting or sleeping our internal body processes are still working and we still use up energy, but at a reduced rate. We may say that our bodies are 'ticking-over' when we are asleep and ready to start work again when required. The rate of tick-over—known by the rather grand name of *basal metabolic rate*—is higher than usual in people with an active thyroid gland which makes a lot of thyroxine. Such people are usually restless, active people. They may eat a lot and still stay thin because their food is burned up comparatively quickly by their bodies and is not converted to body fat. Other people, with less active thyroid glands which make a smaller quantity of thyroxine, are slower and less energetic and they become fat more easily.

113

Obviously iodine is very important in the body and a deficiency of it can have unpleasant results. Fortunately the amounts required are very small—3 g of iodine would be sufficient to last for a lifetime.

★★★ **Keypoint.** Sea foods are the best sources of iodine in the diet. Fish is an excellent source and it provides about one quarter of the iodine in an average diet. Cod liver oil is the richest natural source.

Seaweed contains valuable amounts of iodine, which it collects from the sea water. Seaweed is not very widely eaten, but in some parts of the country it is regarded as a delicacy. In South Wales, for example, cooked seaweed—known as laver bread—has been popular for many years. Even sponges accumulate iodine from sea water although no one has yet gone so far as to eat them!

Where the iodine content of the diet is likely to be small the use of iodized salt is a useful precaution. This contains 1 part of potassium iodide to about 40 000 parts of salt. If the diet contains more iodine than is required the excess is excreted in the urine.

★ ? What are the functions of iron and iodine in the body? What foods are good sources of these two mineral elements?

Calcium. Most of the calcium in our food is used for forming bones and teeth. A small amount of calcium circulates in the blood, which conveys it to and from the bones and teeth. The concentration of calcium in the blood is kept constant, and if there is not enough calcium in our food our bones will be slowly *decalcified*, that is the calcium will be removed from them. The calcium in the bloodstream helps the blood to clot properly and so prevents excessive bleeding from cuts. It also plays a part in the working of nerves and muscles.

The main sources of calcium are shown in the table. Milk, cheese and flour products (mainly bread) supply over four-fifths of the calcium in a British diet.

★★★ **Keypoint.** The best single source of calcium is milk which

SOURCES OF CALCIUM

Type of food	Example	Calcium content (mg/100 g)
Dairy products and eggs	Milk Butter Cheese Eggs	120 15 810 54
Cereals	White bread Flour (70% extraction)	100 138
Vegetables	Cabbage	57
Meat	Beef	7

provides the calcium in a form which is easily digested and absorbed.

★ ? Apart from calcium and phosphorus what other nutrient is required for the formation of healthy bones and teeth?

Fruits and vegetables

Fruits and vegetables are of value as providers of vitamins and mineral elements, though they may supply small amounts of carbohydrates and proteins as well. In general it may be said that fruits are less important than vegetables as a source of vitamins and minerals. In fact fruits may almost be neglected as a source of mineral elements. They do, however, supply valuable amounts of vitamin C, and in an average diet over one-third of this vitamin is supplied by fruits. The energy value of most fruits is small, and this is the main attraction of fruit to some people. Fruit is almost always included in 'slimming diets' because it provides vitamin C without adding greatly to the energy value of the diet. In this way fruit makes up for the reduced vitamin C intake from potatoes which are usually absent from slimming diets.

The importance of fruit and vegetables in the diet is shown in the table on the next page.

★ ? Fruit and vegetables are important in the diet because they supply us with nearly all our intake of one nutrient. What is its name?

THE IMPORTANCE OF FRUIT AND VEGETABLES

	% Contribution to the diet			
	Vitamin A	Vitamin C	Calcium	Iron
Vegetables	23	54	6	22
Potatoes	—	25	1	9
Carrots	16	0·5	—	—
Cabbage, sprouts, cauliflower	1	9	1	2
Fruits	1	32	2	4
Oranges	—	10	—	—
Tomatoes	1	6	—	—

WATER

All living things from the simplest bacteria to the giant oak tree—are made up largely of water and are constantly losing water. As we have seen, our bodies are two-thirds water, and we lose water in our breath, in perspiration and in urine. Obviously the water lost from our bodies must be replaced, or in time we would completely dry up. It is possible for us to live for fairly long periods without food, because our bodies can use up reserves of fat. Although we would get thinner and feel very hungry, we would still be alright while these food reserves lasted. No one can go for very long without water, however, because our bodies—unlike the camel's—do not have a reserve supply.

The water in our bodies acts as a form of water transport. Our blood circulation system—which is mainly composed of water—can be likened to a network of canals, which carries food to the tissues and brings back waste materials, such as carbon dioxide and urea. The carbon dioxide is removed from the blood by the lungs and it is replaced by a supply of oxygen. The urea and excess water in the blood are removed by the kidneys and in this way the blood is 'reconditioned' to carry out its work again. All the tissues of the body are bathed in a watery fluid, and this is regularly renewed by the blood.

Most of us obtain enough water from our food and drink but it is impossible to have too much because any excess over our needs is promptly removed from the blood by the kidneys and excreted in the urine.

116

The top picture shows how rivers may become obviously polluted, in this case by detergent wastes. Even the placid water shown in the bottom picture needs careful treatment before it is fit to drink

Drinking water. The water we drink is not pure because it contains small quantities of dissolved solids and gases. Oxygen, nitrogen and carbon dioxide are picked up when the water falls as rain through the air. In industrial areas sulphur dioxide may also be picked up in the same way. When rain water percolates through the ground it dissolves small quantities of mineral salts—chiefly the sulphates and bicarbonates of calcium and magnesium. When calcium and magnesium compounds are present in water they make it difficult to obtain a lather with soap. Such water is said to be 'hard'. Hard water makes good drinking water because of the dissolved calcium it contains but the amount of calcium our bodies get in this way is quite small. By removing the mineral salts which cause hardness, it is possible to 'soften' hard water so that it will easily form a lather with soap.

Natural water contains dissolved oxygen and also material derived from vegetation and animals. Polluted water supplies may be the cause of diseases such as typhoid fever, cholera and jaundice and in order to purify drinking water it is often treated before use by adding about 1 part of chlorine to 2 000 000 parts of the water.

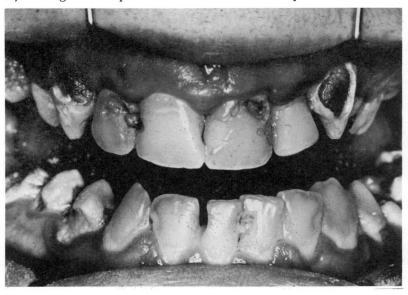

Tooth decay. Nearly all British children suffer from some dental decay. Although fluoridation can help to prevent dental decay in children, proper oral hygiene and attention to the diet are also necessary. Sweet foods are particularly bad for teeth (see page 70)

This kills most of the bacteria, but the chlorine is present in such small amounts that it cannot be tasted.

★★★ **Keypoint.** The presence of small amounts of *fluorine* salts in drinking water is beneficial because it helps to prevent teeth from decaying.

It has been shown by experiments carried out over many years that 1 part of fluoride (salt of fluorine) in 1 000 000 parts of water (1 part per million) is effective in reducing dental decay, especially in young children. In some parts of the U.K.—where the concentration of fluoride in water is lower than this—fluorine salts are added to water to help reduce dental decay. Fluoride toothpastes are also available to supplement fluoride in water supplies.

Beverages

Many people drink little or no water as such but rely on tea, coffee and other drinks to quench their thirst. Our bodies are able to extract the water from these drinks quite efficiently and they serve almost as well as pure water. Tea and coffee have practically no nutritional value in themselves, but the sugar and milk with which they are usually drunk has food value.

Tea. Apart from water and milk, tea is the world's most popular beverage and in Britain we drink more than anyone else. Every year we drink about 5 kg each—which represents about 2500 cups of tea! The tea plant is an evergreen shrub which grows in warm countries such as India, China and Ceylon.

Tea is processed in the following way:

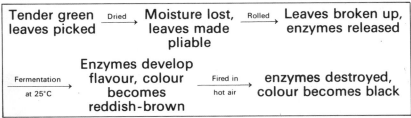

The most important ingredients of tea are *caffeine* and *tannin*. Caffeine has a mild stimulating or pick-me-up action and this is one reason why tea is such a popular drink. Tannin has a bitter taste and a well-made cup of tea should not contain much of it.

119

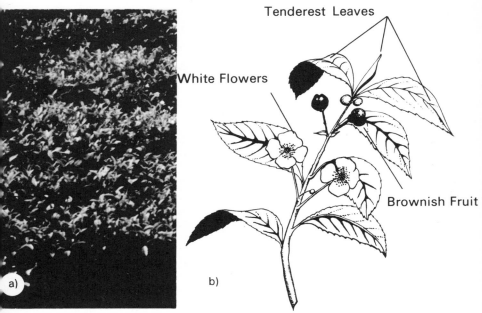

Fig. 37. (a) Part of a tea plantation and (b) a branch of the tea shrub, showing the tenderest leaves, which are the only ones used for making good quality tea

Both caffeine and tannin are extracted from tea leaves by hot water, but tannin is extracted more slowly than caffeine. When tea is allowed to stand in the teapot, more and more tannin is extracted and the tea becomes bitter. This is why a second cup of tea is never as nice as the first. As well as tannin and caffeine, tea contains small amounts of flavouring materials called *essential oils*. It is the essential oils which give high-grade tea its pleasing aroma and delicate taste.

★★ **Activity.** Half fill beakers with (a) hot water (e.g. 70°C), (b) freshly boiled water and (c) water that has been boiled for 5 minutes. Add a tea-bag to each beaker and allow to stand for 1 minute. Remove the tea-bags and observe and taste each tea sample. Note colour, brightness and bitterness. Take a used tea-bag and repeat (b). How has the colour and flavour altered? How do you explain your results?

Coffee. The coffee plant, like the tea plant, is an evergreen shrub which is cultivated in many tropical countries, especially Brazil.

120

The fruit looks like a cherry and contains two seeds or beans enclosed in a tough skin. The beans are dried in air and the skin or husk is removed by rolling.

★★★ **Keypoint.** The caffeine content of coffee beans is only about one-third that of tea. They also contain tannin and a complex mixture of essential oils and other compounds which provide the characteristic coffee flavour.

An African woman picking coffee 'cherries' from mature coffee bushes

As is well known, coffee beans are roasted and ground before use. Ground coffee rapidly loses its flavour if it is allowed to stand in air, and so it should always be stored in an airtight container. The aim of good coffee-making is to extract the maximum amount of flavouring matter and caffeine, and the minimum amount of tannin. Coffee is expensive and chicory—which adds to the colour and the flavour—is often mixed with it to make it cheaper.

★★ **Activity.** Repeat the tea experiment using ground coffee in coffee bags in place of tea bags.

Cocoa. Cocoa trees are grown in many tropical countries, and are somewhat like apple trees both in size and shape. Cocoa beans—from which both cocoa and chocolate are made—grow in large egg-shaped pods (Fig. 38). After harvesting, the pods are split

121

open and the beans scraped out. They are fermented for several days and dried. In making cocoa (and chocolate) the beans are first roasted, and it is this process which causes the well-known chocolate flavour and aroma to develop. After roasting, the beans are broken into small pieces called *nibs* and ground. Grinding turns the nibs into a thick brown liquid which sets into a fatty solid. Some of the fat, which is called *cocoa butter*, is squeezed out, and the solid left is turned into cocoa powder by careful grinding and sieving.

Unlike tea and coffee, cocoa powder is rich in nutrients and contains roughly a fifth protein, a fifth fat and nearly a half carbohydrate. In addition it contains 7 mg/100 g iron and calcium, vitamin A and the B vitamins. When cocoa is drunk as a beverage it is mixed with hot milk and milky cocoa has considerable food value. It also has a mild pick-me-up action because it contains small amounts of the stimulant *theobromine*.

★★ **Activity.** Add one teaspoonful of cocoa to beakers half full of (a) cold water, (b) hot water (e.g. 70°C) and (c) boiling water. Stir well and note the appearance and flavour of each. Boil (c) for two minutes and note any change in appearance and flavour. (Cocoa contains starch.) What is the best way of making cocoa?

★ ? In making tea only the soluble matter is extracted from the tea leaves, but in making cocoa ground beans are present. What difference does this make to its appearance and food value?

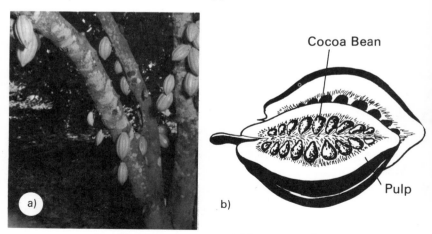

a)

b)

Cocoa Bean

Pulp

Fig. 38. (a) A cocoa tree and (b) a cocoa pod

122

Soft drinks

Soft drinks provide water in a pleasant form, but they differ widely in quality and food value from preserved fruit juices with a useful vitamin C content to artificial carbonated 'fizzy' drinks which may contain little or no fruit and whose food value may be nil except for any sugar present.

★★★ **Keypoint.** A glass of orange juice made from a whole orange contains 50 mg vitamin C; that is more than a day's supply.

The main types of fruit drink are as follows:

1. Fruit squash. At least 25% of the undiluted drink must by law be fruit juice; they contain a little vitamin C.

2. Fruit drinks. At least 10% of the undiluted drink must by law be whole fruit; they are made by liquidizing the whole fruit; they contain a little vitamin C.

3. Fruit cordial. These are fruit squashes that contain no solid matter and are perfectly clear, e.g. lime juice cordial.

4. Fruit-flavoured drinks. May not contain any fruit but only synthetic fruit flavours in which case they contain no vitamin C.

5. Carbonated drinks. These are charged with carbon dioxide gas which is released when the bottle is opened so making them 'fizzy'. They contain no vitamin C.

Water from food. Almost all the solid food we eat contains quite a lot of water. There is more water in some fruits and vegetables than there is in milk. Lettuce, for example, contains about 97% water compared with about 87% in milk. The water content of food which we normally regard as 'dry' food can also be substantial—bread contains about 40% water and eggs about 70%. Most people get between $\frac{1}{2}$–$\frac{3}{4}$ litres of water a day from 'solid' food, and their bodies make use of this in exactly the same way as water from drinks.

★ ? Can you think of any foods that contain no water?

MINERAL ELEMENTS AND WATER SUMMARY

Name	Main sources	Functions in the body and effect of shortage
Sodium	Widely distributed in foods. Sodium chloride is extensively used in cooking and as a condiment	Sodium chloride is present in all the body fluids, and is used for making hydrochloric acid present in gastric juices. Shortage causes cramp
Iron	Bread, flour, meat, liver, potatoes, eggs	Used by the body to make haemoglobin, which is present in the red blood cells. Shortage causes anaemia
Iodine	Drinking water, fish, fish liver oil, iodized salt, milk and cereals	The body uses iodine to make thyroxine which regulates the rate at which the body functions. Absence or shortage causes goitre
Calcium	Bread, flour, milk and cheese	Used for the formation of bones and teeth and is also present in the blood. Shortage severely affects the bones, which become soft and weak. It is also necessary for the proper clotting of the blood and the normal functioning of the muscles
Water	Drinking water, tea, coffee, milk, vegetables, fruits and most foods	Water is the medium in which the body's thousand and one reactions occur. It is used for transporting nutrients and waste materials to and from the tissues. The body cannot tolerate a shortage of water for any length of time

7 Meal Planning and a Balanced Diet

★ ? What are the three main functions of food?

In the last three chapters we have discussed which foods carry out these functions and you will no doubt be able to think of some foods which carry out all three of these functions in the body. Milk, for example, is one of the most valuable foods in our diet for it contains every class of nutrient. Yet you would not remain healthy very long if your diet consisted of nothing but milk, for though it contains both mineral elements and vitamins, it contains very little *iron* and *vitamin D*.

In other words milk is not a *perfect* food because it does not contain all the essential nutrients in the proportions needed by our bodies. There is no single food known which is a perfect food, and it follows that a satisfactory diet must be based not on one, but on several foods.

★★★ **Keypoint.** A satisfactory diet is one that will supply us with all our needs. We often call this a *balanced diet*; that is one which supplies us with *all* the essential nutrients and which contains them in the *correct proportions* for our needs.

There are lots of different ways of making a balanced diet, and that is why planning meals is so interesting. It is possible to work out balanced diets based on only a few foods. For instance, a diet based on three foods—milk, wholemeal bread and green vegetables—would be satisfactory from a nutritional point of view, though it would not be very exciting! There is also the danger that if we try to use only a few foods the diet will not be balanced. For example, in the last century the diet of the poorer people of Ireland was based mainly on a single food—the potato. Potatoes are a valuable food, but a diet based on them will be a mainly starchy

Many people in India have a monotonous diet based on one main food such as rice; these diets are very unbalanced. Is your diet balanced or do you eat too much of any one food?

diet and though it might provide enough energy it would not provide enough of some other nutrients.

★★★ **Keypoint.** In general, although it is *possible* to plan balanced diets based on only a few foods, it is much better to use as wide a variety of foods as possible.

Recommended daily amounts of nutrients

In planning a diet, we must think of the needs of the person who is going to live on it. It is fairly obvious, for example, that a diet which suits a farm worker would be disastrous for a baby! In Great Britain we have as a guide a set of recommended amounts of each nutrient for various types of people. If you turn back to

126

Fig. 18 on page 44 you will see how energy needs vary with occupation. Energy needs also vary according to whether a person is slim or fat, whether they are old or young and so on. Protein allowances are calculated on the basis of our energy needs, and very roughly we can say that in a balanced diet protein should supply adults with at least 10% of their energy.

★★ **Activity.** A fairly active man requires 12 000 kJ/day. How many kilojoules should protein provide? If the energy value of protein is 17 kJ/g, what should the daily protein intake be? Check your answer against Fig. 39.

There is a recommended intake for each essential nutrient, and you will be able to get some idea of some of these for a typical family from Fig. 39.

Kilojoules	12 000	9000	8250	3700
g Protein	72	54	49	22
g Calcium	0·5	0·5	0·6	0·6
g Iron	0·01	0·012	0·01	0·006
g Vitamin C	0·03	0·03	0·02	0·015
	Father, age 18–34 fairly active	**Mother,** age 18–54 active housewife	**Boy,** 7–9 years old	**Baby,** 6–9 months

Fig. 39. Recommended daily amounts of some nutrients for members of a typical family

★ ? What is a balanced diet and why is it best to eat as wide a variety of foods as you can?

127

Foods and a balanced diet

It is no good knowing how much of each nutrient we should have for good health unless we also know which foods in the diet supply us with particular nutrients. For example, you cannot plan a diet that will supply 75 g of protein daily as recommended for an active male worker, unless you know how much protein each food in the diet supplies. To know this we can use *food composition tables,* which tell us the nutrient content of every food. If you look at Fig. 28 on page 75 you will soon be able to plan a day's meals that will contain 75 g of protein.

A diet is, of course, made up of meals, and so by using food tables, we can calculate exactly how much of each nutrient we obtain from a meal. At this point you may be thinking that meal planning seems rather like an unpleasant exercise in arithmetic! In case you have got this impression, it should be said that normally it is quite unnecessary to calculate the exact nutrient content of each meal. It is enough if you know the main nutrients in each food, so that you can check if a meal contains roughly balanced amounts of nutrients. For example, Fig. 40 shows you the portions of various foods that supply 420 kilojoules (or 100 Calories), and you can see at a glance which of these foods you should include in a meal planned to give plenty of energy.

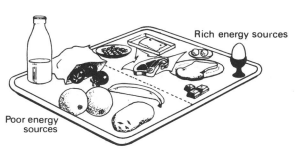

Fig. 40. Portions of food that supply 420 kilojoules (100 Calories)

Rich sources	
Butter,	14 g
Chocolate,	17 g
Beef,	32 g
Cheese,	24 g
Sugar,	25 g
Eggs,	60 g

Poor sources	
Bananas,	140 g
Potatoes,	140 g
Milk,	155 g
Oranges,	280 g
Tomatoes,	700 g

★★★ **Keypoint.** Butter, sugar, chocolate and cheese are concentrated sources of energy, while tomatoes, oranges and bananas are poor sources.

★ ? Which of the foods shown in Fig. 40 is the most concentrated source of energy? Which is the least concentrated?

128

We can now go on to consider how to plan a balanced and varied diet in terms of meals. Before we do this we must point out that sometimes it *is* necessary to calculate the nutrient content of each meal. For example, if you have tried to slim you will know that you have to check your energy intake if you really want to get slimmer. Also, in hospitals it is often necessary to give patients special diets, and this may involve exact calculation of its nutrient content (this is a job usually done by a dietitian).

Food tables and meal planning

(1) You look up dried peas in a Food Table and you are amazed at their high food content. They are a good energy source, rich in protein and contain useful amounts of vitamin B_1. You resolve to use plenty of dried peas in the meals you are planning, and you conclude that dried peas must make a substantial contribution to the diet. Right or wrong? Wrong both times! First, we eat peas after cooking when their water content increases by 60%. Their food value expressed *per unit weight* therefore falls, and their nutrient content looks much less impressive. Second, peas don't make a big contribution to our diet simply because we don't eat large quantities. The contribution of all pulses (peas, beans and lentils) to an average diet is as follows:

0.2% of the energy
0.6% of the protein
1.4% of the vitamin B_1

(2) Compared with fresh peas the food value of potatoes is small. Old potatoes have a fairly small energy value (see Fig. 40), contain little protein (2%) and little vitamin C. Yet because we eat so many potatoes—on average about 1 kg/week—potatoes contribute much more to the diet than peas, namely:

5% of the energy
4% of the protein
25% of the vitamin C

(3) Liver is rich in iron (14 mg/100 g), potatoes are poor in iron (0.7 mg/100 g), but potatoes are a much better source of iron in the average diet than liver because we eat plenty of potatoes but little liver. In fact potatoes contribute 9% of the iron in our diet, liver only 3%.

★★★ Keypoint. In deciding which foods are good sources of a particular nutrient in the diet you must take into account not only the food value as given in tables but also the amounts normally eaten.

★ ? The vitamin C content of blackcurrants is 200 mg/100 g and that of old potatoes 10 mg/100 g; which of these two foods do you think is the better source of vitamin C in an ordinary diet? Why?

% CONTRIBUTIONS MADE BY IMPORTANT GROUPS TO AN AVERAGE BRITISH DIET

Food group	Energy	Protein	Fat	Calcium	Iron
Milk, cheese, eggs	17	30	23	63	10
Meat, fish	17	32	28	4	25
Cereals	29	25	10	22	33
Fruits, vegetables	10	10	2	8	25
Fats	15	—	36	—	—
Sugar, preserves	10	—	—	—	1

In considering the average British diet it is convenient to group the wide variety of foodstuffs consumed into six main categories, namely; (1) milk, cheese and eggs, (2) meat and fish, (3) cereals, (4) fruits and vegetables, (5) fats and (6) sugar and preserves. It is true that not all the items of our diet are included within these groups but excluded items, such as beverages, make a tiny contribution to the diet as a whole. The contribution of these food groups to the energy, proteins, fat, calcium and iron in an average British diet is shown in the table above, and their contribution to vitamins in the table opposite.

The importance of the group containing milk, cheese and eggs is evident from these tables and of this group fresh milk makes by far the greatest contribution providing 11% of the energy, 18% of the protein, 14% of the fat, 47% of the calcium and 34% of the vitamin B_2 in an average diet. Meat and fish make a major contribution to all the nutrients shown in the tables except calcium and vitamin C. These two groups of foods account for half the cost of an average diet and provide it with one-third of its energy, half its fat and nearly two-thirds of its proteins as well as making major contributions to mineral elements and vitamins, with the big exception of vitamin C.

130

% VITAMIN CONTRIBUTIONS TO AN AVERAGE BRITISH DIET

Food group	Vitamin A	Vitamin B$_1$	Vitamin B$_2$	Vitamin C	Vitamin D
Milk, cheese, eggs	23	16	48	9	31
Meat, fish	23	15	19	1	19
Cereals	1	44	7	—	6
Fruits, vegetables	24	22	10	86	—
Fats	26	1	1	—	43
Sugar, preserves	—	—	—	2	—

The importance of cereals (mainly bread) is evident from the tables, and as has been noted before they supply nearly one-third of our energy intake. The importance of fruit and vegetables as a main source of the vitamins in our diet (especially vitamin C) is also clear from the tables (see page 116 for further details).

★ ? Apart from their importance as an energy source, why are fats important in the diet? Could we do without sugar and preserves?

How to plan meals

In planning an attractive balanced meal the following general principles should be followed. The meal should contain foods which are rich in protein and foods which are rich in mineral elements and vitamins. Once these requirements have been met, enough energy-giving food should be included to satisfy the appetite. The meal should also include enough different foods to make it interesting, and these should be cooked and served so as to make the various dishes as attractive as possible.

Using the idea of the six food groups mentioned above, and noting the nutrients they supply from the tables, it is easy to draw up some general guidelines to planning meals. This is done in the table on the next page.

Meals should not be planned one at a time; to achieve a balanced diet plan a complete day's meals—or better a complete week's meals—at a time.

★★★ **Keypoint.** While including items from each food group use as many *different* foods as possible.

THE MAIN FOOD GROUPS AND THEIR USE IN MEAL PLANNING

Group 1	
Milk	Include some (preferably a pint) daily; extra for children and expectant and nursing mothers
Cheese	Include several times a week; a concentrated cheap source of protein
Eggs	At least three times a week
Group 2	
Meat and Fish	Once a day unless plenty of group 1 foods are eaten
Group 3	
Cereals	As required to satisfy hunger; include some bread each day
Group 4	
Fruit	Some fruit each day; citrus fruit are especially valuable for vitamin C
Vegetables	Potatoes and one other daily; should be cooked carefully or eaten raw
Group 5	
Fats	Include enough to make foods palatable and to satisfy appetite
Group 6	
Sugar and Preserves	Include enough to make food palatable but in general use as little as possible

★ ? In addition to the solid foods mentioned in the six groups, what else should be included in meals?

Some well-balanced meals

Using the general principles discussed above, we can plan meals that are well-balanced, varied and attractive. Here is such a set of menus for a day.

Breakfast   Fresh or tinned fruit; egg, bacon and fried bread; toast, butter and marmalade; tea.

This meal has body-building foods (egg, bread and bacon), varied mineral elements and vitamins (fruit, butter, egg,

Do you think this breakfast would be more suitable for an office worker or a coal miner?
Why?

bacon and bread) and energy foods (mainly toast and fried bread, but also butter and marmalade). By eating plenty of toast and fried bread, large appetites may be satisfied.

Morning snack

Milky coffee (or milk) with sugar; biscuits.
    Most people enjoy a short break from work and a light snack during the morning, and this is quite a good habit from a nutritional point of view, especially for children and heavy manual workers. The snack suggested provides body-building nutrients (milk and biscuits), mineral elements (milk and biscuits) and energy foods (sugar, milk, biscuits).

Lunch

Meat or fish, potatoes and peas; stewed fruit and custard; water.
    For many people lunch is the main meal of the day and it should be planned so as to be a satisfying meal. The lunch above contains body-building material (mainly meat or fish and potatoes, also milk in the custard, and peas), vitamins and mineral elements (mainly fruit, also to a less extent the other items of the meal, except water), and energy foods (mainly meat and potatoes, also peas and milk and sugar in

133

the custard). It is good practice to include water with one meal; the body needs at least two to three pints a day, and more does no harm.

High tea   *Cheese salad; bread, butter and jam; cakes; tea.*
        This meal has body-building nutrients (mainly cheese, also bread and cakes), mineral elements and vitamins (mainly salad, also bread, butter and cakes) and energy-giving nutrients (mainly bread, butter, jam and cakes).

Bed-time   *Hot milk (flavoured if desired in the form of chocolate or Ovaltine);*
snack   *Ryvita, butter, honey.*
        Before going to bed most people enjoy a light snack, and this one contains body-building nutrients (milk and Ryvita), mineral elements and vitamins (milk, Ryvita and butter) and energy (milk, Ryvita, butter and honey).

★★ **Activity.** Plan a complete day's meals for yourself. If possible prepare and eat them. Do you consider the breakfast shown on page 133 suitable for a manual worker? If not, what would you add?

Some badly planned meals

Lunch 1   *Potato soup; cornish pasties (mainly meat and potatoes in pastry), fried potatoes; steamed jam pudding; tea.*
        If you had this lunch you should feel full of carbohydrate, but you would not be full of much else! This meal is badly balanced because it contains far too much starchy material, and very little of body-building or other value.

Lunch 2   *Chicken soup; mixed grill consisting of lamb chop, kidney and sausage, creamed potatoes; sweet omelette (made from eggs, milk, butter and jam); white coffee.*
        This meal should 'build you a fine body', but it contains far too much protein at the expense of other nutrients.

Lunch 3   *Tomato juice; green salad with lettuce, tomatoes, cucumber, beetroot and celery; fresh fruit salad; tea.*
        This would be a bad meal for a hard day's work; it provides little energy or body-building material, and contains more vitamins and mineral elements than are needed at one time.

★★ **Activity.** Each of the three lunch menus just described is badly balanced because it is based mainly on foods with the same func-

134

Do you think this is a well-balanced main course for an active young person?
What else would you include in the meal?

tion. If you study the menus you will see that by re-arranging
them you can plan three well-balanced and varied meals. Try it!

Planning attractive meals

It is no good planning a well-balanced meal if, when it is prepared,
it is so unattractive that no one will eat it! The following points
should help you in planning meals that are pleasing and satisfying.

The 'top ten' points for attractive satisfying meals
  1. You will know the phrase 'A little of what you fancy does you
      good', but like most such popular sayings it is not always true.
      Very often it *is* a good idea to give people what they like. This

is not *always* true, however, especially where people have been used to bad feeding habits. For example, children who have been brought up to eat as many sweets as they like may develop a craving for sweet foods. Thus if they are always given what they fancy they may choose sweet (energy) foods at the expense of body-building and other foods (see page 70).

2. A meal should *look* nice; it should be freshly prepared and served so that it looks at its best. If the food is a drab colour, its appearance can be improved by adding colour, perhaps in the form of red paprika or a coloured sauce or a gravy containing 'browning'. A coloured decoration—such as a cherry, a sprig of mint or parsley, a slice of orange or tomato—may also be used to improve its appearance.

3. A meal should *smell* good. An appetizing aroma is not only pleasant in itself but it stimulates the flow of digestive juices and makes digestion easier. This is one reason for starting a meal with a good-smelling soup.

4. A meal should be *interesting*. If the same food appears twice in a meal (even if it is disguised on its second appearance!) interest is lost. Interest and variety can be obtained by including food with strong flavour alongside those with little flavour and by mixing crisp foods with soft ones.

5. Meals should take account of the *season* of the year. In hot weather cold dishes—vegetable and fruit salads, cold beverages and sweets—should be provided, while in cold weather hot sustaining foods are in demand.

6. Meals should contain some *dietary fibre*. Baked beans, whole cereals, bread (especially wholemeal), fruit and vegetables all contain fibre. Although it cannot be digested, fibre prevents constipation and keeps us healthy.

★★★ **Keypoint.** Texture, colour and flavour are all important in meal planning and are discussed in Chapter 12.

7. All meals should provide a reasonable amount of *water*. Ideally water itself is best (it may be iced in hot weather) but it may be provided in the form of hot beverages or sauces. Sauces are particularly valuable with meals which would otherwise be rather dry. Fruit and vegetables are also useful sources of water.

8. Both *animal* and *vegetable* protein should be included in meals. For reasons already discussed (Chapter 5) animal protein foods (meat, fish, cheese) should be mixed with vegetable protein foods (potatoes, cakes and bread).

★ ? As far as proteins are concerned 'little and often' is a better slogan than 'plenty now and then'. Why is this?

9. Meals should be eaten in *cheerful* and *relaxing* surroundings.

10. Meals should be eaten with *clean* and attractive utensils. Chipped or cracked crockery and stained or scratched cutlery are both unsightly and unhygienic, and should never be used. Crockery, cutlery and tablecloths should all be clean.

★★★ **Keypoint.** In planning meals the first priority is to make them well balanced. First plan for body-building foods, then for vitamins and mineral elements and finally fill up with energy foods to satisfy the appetite. Ensure variety by choosing food from all six food groups. Then check the 'Top Ten' points above to make sure the meals are attractive.

Value for money

HOW WE SPEND MONEY ON FOOD

Food group	Foods	% of total money spent
Group 1	Milk	9
	Cheese	3
	Eggs	4
Group 2	Meat	33
	Fish	4
Group 3	Bread	6
	Other cereals	9
Group 4	Fruit	6
	Potatoes	3
	Other vegetables	9
Group 5	Fats	5
Group 6	Sugar	2
	Preserves	1

The table on page 137 shows how we spend money on food. In terms of value for money the three staple foods, milk, potatoes and bread are outstanding:

% **money spent** Total %	**Milk 9%; Potatoes, 3%; Bread, 6%.** **18%.**
% **contribution to diet**	**Protein, 38%; Calcium, 62%; Energy, 30%; Vitamin B_1, 47%; Vitamin B_2, 40%; Vitamin C, 33%.**

★★★ **Keypoint.** No other foods match the basic three—milk, potatoes and bread—in terms of food value for money spent. To think of bread and potatoes merely as cheap energy foods is quite wrong!

In terms of food value for money spent meat is very expensive. It is true we need animal protein in our diet, but by careful planning we can make considerable savings in money spent on meat without sacrifice of food value. It is important to realize that food value of meat is not always related to cost. Cheaper cuts of meat will be of poorer quality than expensive ones—they will be less tender and perhaps of less good flavour—but by careful preparation and cooking (see Chapter 11) they can often make just as attractive meals as more expensive cuts.

★★ **Activity.** In your visit to the butchers (page 93) what were your conclusions as to the 'best buy' for beef? All beef is relatively expensive; try and find out how you could get better value for money by selecting other types of meat.

★★ **Activity.** Compare the relative costs of the following pairs and decide which is the 'best buy' in each case: (a) stewing steak and rump steak, (b) leg of lamb and leg of pork, (c) roasting chicken and lamb chops, (d) stewing veal and breast of veal. Remember that some cuts contain a high proportion of bone or fat, and you should take this into account when deciding the best buy.

Even cheap meat may not be the best choice of animal protein in terms of value for money. Fish can often provide a cheaper alternative as no doubt you discovered when you visited a fish-mongers (page 97). Herrings and kippers are often good buys. At the moment we spend only 4% of our total food bill on fish; if we spent more on cheaper varieties of fish and less on expensive cuts of meat we could cut our food bills without any loss of food value.

Cheese is an excellent source of animal protein and very good value for money, yet we only spend 3% of our food bill on it. We should eat more!

★★ **Activity.** Plan six attractive and nutritious dishes using cheese as your main body-building food.

Green vegetables and fresh fruit tend to be expensive but even so they are often good value for money because of the mineral elements and vitamins they provide. They are also invaluable for the interest they can (if properly cooked and served) give to a meal in terms of texture, colour and flavour. Oranges and tomatoes and (in season) carrots and cabbage are usually good buys. On the other hand many luxury fruits and vegetables, such as frozen strawberries, asparagus tips and melons are poor value for money in terms of food value.

Nowadays we are spending more and more on convenience foods and these are expensive in terms of food value. We shall discuss this further in the next chapter.

Economy in meal planning cannot be carried too far, because the cheapest foods are usually starchy foods. Good protein foods—meat, fish, eggs, cheese, milk—are more expensive than starchy ones, and so enough money should be spent on food to ensure that a balanced diet is obtained.

★★★ **Keypoint.** Good meals need not be *expensive*. Efficient meal planning should be economic in the sense that it provides balanced nutrients and variety at minimum cost.

Meals for the very young

For the first few months of its life a baby is breast-fed on its mother's milk. After about six months the baby should be gradually weaned and spoon-feeding started. As mother's milk is replaced by cow's milk extra vitamin C (usually from orange juice) and vitamin A and D (usually from cod liver oil) should be provided as cow's milk is not a rich source of these vitamins. Sometimes babies have to be bottle-fed from birth, in which case the diluted cow's milk used must always be supplemented with orange juice and cod liver oil. Cow's milk is also lacking in iron

Milk is the basis of diet for the very young. Between the ages of 1–5 at least a pint of milk should be included in the diet every day

and as soon as possible after spoon-feeding has been started, solid foods containing iron should be introduced. Sieved green vegetables, minced meats and mashed hard-boiled eggs are all suitable for this purpose.

Between the ages of one and two the baby's teeth are developing and the change from a liquid milk diet to a normal-type diet is completed. To encourage the baby to use its teeth crisp foods, such as rusks and thin toast, should be added to the diet.

After its second birthday the child's diet resembles that of an adult, except that the amounts eaten are small and meals should be rich in body-building and protective foods. At this stage milk should still be the basis of the diet, and at least a pint a day should be included. Rich foods that are difficult to digest, such as fried foods and rich cakes, and twice-cooked foods should be avoided.

Meals for school-children

The years spent at school are the time of rapid growth and change in our bodies. It follows that meals for school-children must provide for these needs. The amounts of body-building foods needed by the body is at its greatest during this period, and the diet should therefore supply plenty of protein and calcium. Apart from calcium the diet should contain plenty of foods rich in other mineral elements and also vitamins. In particular girls should be given plenty of iron-rich foods—meat (especially liver and kidney), green vegetables and bread—during puberty.

The early teens is a period of great physical activity and therefor of hearty appetites. School-children should eat as much energy-giving food as they feel like, and it is good practice to include plenty of fatty foods in the diet, as these are concentrated sources of energy.

Substantial, simple and well-cooked meals are the best for school-children. Plenty of the staple foods—bread, milk and potatoes—should be provided, along with substantial amounts of meat or fish, cheese, butter or margarine, green vegetables and fresh fruit.

Meals for adults

When we stop growing, our appetites get less because our need for food gets less. Of course we still need a balanced diet when we are fully grown, and the principles of good meal-planning already discussed should be followed.

People who are doing heavy manual work should be given more energy-rich foods than people doing only light work, and so their diets should be rich in potatoes, bread, cereals, sugar, milk and fat. Large servings ot these carbohydrate-rich foods may be given. Hot fried meals are more desirable for such people than salads, because they are more sustaining and richer in energy.

The amount of vitamins and mineral elements needed by the body does not vary with occupation and so both heavy and light workers should be given the same amounts.

141

Women have smaller energy needs than men and so their appetites are smaller. Although women should be given less of energy-rich foods than men, they should be given the same amounts of vitamins and mineral elements. In particular expectant and nursing mothers should be given plenty of foods which supply vitamins and mineral elements.

Meals for invalids

If you have ever been kept in bed for weeks—or even days—on end, you will know just how important meals are to an invalid. They need especial care in planning, cooking and serving.

Invalids suffering from some diseases—such as diabetes and anaemia—need special diets, and in such cases the doctor will advise what foods should be eaten. Apart from this, diets for invalids should follow certain simple rules:

1. If the invalid has a higher than normal temperature, the diet should consist of liquids only. The main items on the diet should be milk, milk beverages and jellies; nourishing soups and fruit drinks.
2. Invalids with near-normal temperatures need a light diet with only small amounts of energy-foods. Milk, eggs, fish, green vegetables and plenty of fruit should be given.
3. All the foods in the diet should be served in an easily-digestible form and should not require too much chewing. Milk drinks, milk puddings and jellies; steamed fish with a tasty sauce; stewed and minced meat; lightly cooked egg dishes; these are all suitable.
4. Foods which are difficult to digest or eat—fried foods, tough meat, rich cakes—should not be given.
5. As invalids are nursed back to health, the amount of vitamins and mineral elements in the diet should be increased. Fresh fruit is particularly suitable, and if this is not available bottled or canned fruit juices may be used.
6. Plenty of variety should be the aim of meal planning, and as the range of desirable foods is limited, special attention should be given to the provision of tasty sauces, and a good variety of beverages and soups.
7. Food should be fresh and of good quality and served imme-

The 'Meals on Wheels' service showing food being taken out of containers in which it has been kept hot

diately after cooking. It should be served as attractively as possible.

8. Although servings should be small, meals should be frequent and regular.

Meals for the elderly

Elderly people are more likely to suffer from poor food and an unbalanced diet than younger more active people for the following reasons:

1. They are often lonely and so don't bother to spend much time on preparing or eating food.
2. They often don't enjoy their food very much because of a reduced sense of taste and smell.

3. They often don't have the energy to prepare attractive meals.
4. They often find it difficult to chew and digest food properly and so they select soft carbohydrate foods in preference to protein foods such as meat and fish.
5. Their income is often low and so they spend too little on food. The result may be an unbalanced diet with too many cheap starchy foods and not enough protein foods or fruit and vegetables.
6. Many elderly people don't understand the principles of meal planning and so have an unbalanced diet.

★ ? The diet of some old people is low in vitamin C, B vitamins and iron. Why is this and what foods should be added to their diet to improve the intake of these nutrients?

The 'Meals on Wheels' service (see photograph on page 143) has been designed to make sure that old folk get at least one nutritious well-balanced meal a day (sometimes the service can only call once or twice a week). Meals are cooked in a central kitchen and kept hot in mobile vans which deliver the meal direct to the old person's home.

★ ? If meals on wheels are kept hot for too long in their containers or if they are kept hot for some time after they have been delivered, what nutrients might be lost?

Meals for vegetarians

Strict vegetarians will eat no food that is of animal origin. This means that meat, fish, eggs, milk, cheese and butter cannot be used. Planning a balanced diet for such people is rather like planning a journey for someone who will not travel by air, road or rail!

One difficulty in planning a diet for such people is that as animal protein cannot be used, there is little prospect of including protein of high nutritional value in the diet except for foods made from soya beans. It is also difficult to provide enough mineral elements, such as calcium and iron, and fat-soluble vitamins (vitamin A and D). Even the use of soya bean foods and other nutritious foods, such as nuts and margarine, cannot prevent such a diet from being *very* bulky. It will tend to be unbalanced, with too many energy-giving foods and too few body-building foods.

144

This vegetarian meal consists of vegetable soup, wholemeal bread with nut butter, tomato juice, water, nut rissoles with boiled potato and salad, fresh fruit and nuts.
★? Would you regard this as a balanced meal for (a) a housewife and (b) a heavy manual worker? Give your reasons

Fortunately not many vegetarians are strict, and most of them only exclude animal *flesh* from the diet and continue to eat such animal *products* as milk, eggs and cheese. As you can see from the table on page 130 these group 1 foods contribute nearly a third of the protein in an average diet as well as mineral elements and vitamins. In the absence of meat and fish in the diet they are even more valuable as sources of these nutrients and with their help it is no longer difficult to plan a well-balanced diet. Such vegetarian diets need not be bulky and they do not differ greatly from a 'normal' diet, except that no use is made of fish and meat and to compensate in some measure for this, nuts and soya foods are used.

Packed meals

Some people suppose that a packed meal always has less nutritional value than a cooked one. This is quite wrong! By careful

145

planning and preparation a packed meal may be nutritious, well-balanced, full of variety and attractive.

Bread—in the form of sandwiches or rolls—usually forms the basis of packed meals. For the sake of variety non-sweet biscuits and crisp breads, such as Ryvita, may also be used. These are spread with butter and filled with a variety of fillings. Ham and pineapple, cheese and cucumber, egg and tomato, sardines and lettuce are all nutritious and attractive. The combination of bread, butter and filling if well planned can have nutritional value equal to that of a hot 'meat and two veg' course.

Packed meals should include either raw vegetables or fresh fruit, and milk or coffee. The beverage may be either iced or hot according to the season if a vacuum flask is available. Hungry people may be satisfied by the inclusion of sweet biscuits or cake.

SLIMMING

It is fashionable nowadays to be slim, and popular magazines are full of suggestions of how to slim easily. Apart from fashion, many people are too fat, and this is undesirable as it puts a big strain on the heart and other organs.

Why do we become fat?

> Jack Sprat could eat no fat
> His wife could eat no lean:
> But just the same they both got fat,
> Strange as this may seem.

The simple answer to our question is that we grow fat when the energy input to our bodies from food exceeds our energy output. In this connection it is important to realize that—as suggested by the rhyme above—it is not only fatty foods which contribute to fat build-up in the body. The body is not particular as to whether it uses carbohydrates or fats or proteins as its energy source; whatever the source, excess energy food is converted into fat within the body. It is a simple and perhaps unwelcome fact that we get fat

Packed meals can be attractive and nutritious. *Top*. Crisp French bread spread with grilled bacon, scrambled egg and sausage slices. *Bottom*. Three-decker sandwiches filled with chicken, scrambled egg and tomato.

because our energy intake is too high—or more bluntly because we eat too much.

The reasons given above as to why people grow fat are very simple but like so many simple things they do not represent the complete truth. It is too simple to suggest that any one theory of obesity can be applied to everyone. The simple explanation is satisfactory enough for most people, but it does not seem to apply to those who do not grow fat however much they eat. It is believed that people who do not grow fat easily, have a mechanism inside their bodies which acts as a sort of regulator; if they eat only a little, the regulator slows down the rate at which the body uses up energy. As they eat more, so the regulator causes the body to increase the rate at which it uses up energy and in this way they are able to use up any extra food and so do not grow fat.

Results of recent research suggest that those people who do grow fat easily have difficulty in converting carbohydrate into energy in their bodies. Such people convert carbohydrate into fat rather than into energy. Fortunately they can convert fat and protein into energy without difficulty so it is not that they do not gain enough energy from food, but just that they do not use carbohydrate for energy. Although people who grow fat easily may consider themselves unlucky, they can be thankful that as we now understand the reason, we can plan diets that will enable them to remain slim.

Meals for slimming

There are many ways of trying to slim but, because obesity is caused by too high an intake of energy foods, the most obvious way is to change one's eating habits in some way. In fact about 80% of slimmers say that they have made such a change. The different ways that they used are shown in the table opposite.

An ideal slimming diet should enable the slimmer to eat as much as he or she likes. But for this to be possible a careful selection of the foods to be eaten is essential. The use of the term 'slimming diet' is perhaps unwise, because it makes you think of foods being weighed and energy units counted whereas the whole idea is that meals for slimming should be as normal as possible. It is likely that the most satisfactory diet—and one that does not involve tedious weighing and calculating—is that which limits intake of carbohydrate while allowing unlimited intake of fat and protein. Some

CHANGES MADE IN FOOD HABITS BY SLIMMERS
(based on a poll of 2000 people)

Change made	Men (%)	Women (%)
Eat less	17	14
Eat less starchy foods	80	85
Eat less or cut out sugar	20	20
Eat more fruit	9	12
Cut down on fluids	10	5
Eat special slimming foods	13	14

slimming diets cut down on both carbohydrate and fat, but a low-fat diet is unpalatable to many people and cutting down on carbohydrate alone is therefore more satisfactory. The latter plan carries the added bonus that cutting down carbohydrate is likely to be accompanied by some reduction in fat consumption, e.g. if

THE CARBOHYDRATE CONTENT OF FOODS

Type of food	Carbo-hydrate	Examples (carbohydrate as % of total weight)
Cereal foods	High	Sweet biscuits (66), Cake (60) Bread (50), Energen rolls (46)
Sugar and preserves	High	Sugar (100), Toffee (71), Jam (70), Chocolate (53)
Milk products and eggs	Low	Milk (5), Double cream (2), Butter (0), Cheese (0), Eggs (0)
Meat and fish	Low	Meat (0), Fish (0), Bacon (0), Sausages (10)
Fruit	Low	Apples (10), Oranges (10), Plums (10), Grapefruit (5), Lemons (3)
	Medium	Grapes (15), Bananas (20)
	High	Dates (64), Raisins (64)
Vegetables	Low	Peas (10), Brussels Sprouts (5), Onions (5), Cabbage (5), Tomatoes (3), Runner beans (3), Lettuce (2), Mushrooms (trace)
	Medium	Potatoes (20)

you cut down on bread, consumption of butter is likely to be reduced as well.

The second merit of the low-carbohydrate diet is that it is the most desirable type for those who grow fat easily because their bodies convert carbohydrate to fat rather than energy.

The popularity of the low-carbohydrate diet is evident from the fact most people who slim by changing their eating habits cut down carbohydrate by eating less starchy foods and/or sugar (see the table on page 149).

★ ? About 10% of people who change their eating habits in order to slim eat additional fruit, and this is a good idea. Why?

The table on page 149 gives a guide as to what sort of foods should be avoided in low-carbohydrate meals. The foods which should be most severely cut are sugar and sugar-rich foods such as sweets and jam. Plan slimming meals as follows:

Food group		How much to cut down
Group 6	Sugar and preserves	Most severely
Group 5	Fats	Severely
Group 3	Cereals	Severely unless rich in fibre
Group 4	Fruit and vegetables	Eat plenty except for those with high energy value
Group 1	Milk, cheese, eggs	Eat plenty of cheese and eggs, restrict milk unless skimmed
Group 2	Lean meat and fish	Eat as much as you like

★★ **Activity.** Plan a day's meals for yourself that will reduce your energy intake, but not your intake of body-building or protective nutrients. Calculate its approximate energy content.

★★★ **Keypoint.** Include fibre-rich foods in meals for slimming. They have low energy value. Baked beans on toast is an ideal snack; it is low in energy, medium in protein and high in fibre. Fibre is useful because it is very filling but has a low energy value.

8 Convenience Foods

No doubt if you live in a town you now take the supermarket for granted, yet it has revolutionized our lives! Year by year more and more self-service shops and supermarkets are opening and now we are seeing the development of the super-supermarket or *hypermarket*. In the last 10 years the number of self-service stores and supermarkets in the U.K. has almost doubled, and there are now over 33 000.

The rapid advance of supermarkets has only been possible because of new developments in the types of food product that are available. Products need to be pre-weighed and pre-packed so that they can be distributed and handled easily; they must have a reasonably long *shelf life*, which means that they must remain in perfect condition during storage in the store and also in the home; they must also be attractive and be packaged in such a way as to have 'eye-appeal'. They must also have one other important property; they must be convenient to use. This is why they have been given the name *Convenience Foods*.

★★★ **Keypoint.** What are the advantages of the self-service type of store? We can list them as follows:

1. Competitive prices.
2. Very wide variety.
3. Easy choice and comparison of goods.
4. Guaranteed freshness.
5. High standards of hygiene.
6. Good shopping conditions.

One thing is certain—we are gradually buying more and more foods from supermarkets, and many of these are convenience foods. In particular we are eating more and more frozen foods; indeed sales of frozen food are increasing more rapidly than those of any other type. The range of convenience foods is increasing all the time—every item that you can see in the picture on page 152 is a convenience food.

A Modern Supermarket. Every food you can see is a convenience food

★★★ **Keypoint.** What are convenience foods? They are foods that have been *processed* in some way in a factory to reduce or eliminate the amount of preparation and cooking that they require in the home. They are usually sold in packets, bottles or cans.

★★ **Activity.** Write down all you had to eat yesterday. How many of these items were convenience foods?

Many convenience foods have been preserved in some way and it is certain that the shelves of supermarkets would be almost empty if all preserved foods were removed. It is hard to think of any type of food that has not been preserved in some way: fruit, vegetables, meat, fish, cereals and so on—all are available in a variety of preserved and convenience forms.

Before we can understand modern methods of food preservation we need to know why food goes bad.

Why food goes bad

The most important cause of food spoilage is attack by small creatures known as *micro-organisms* which spoil the food and make it unattractive to humans. Individual micro-organisms are invisible to the naked eye and are smaller than the smallest speck of dust. The micro-organisms may be *moulds, yeasts* or *bacteria*.

Moulds. Have you seen moulds growing on food that is old? For example, bread will quickly become mouldy if kept for more than

152

a few days. Strange as it may seem, the fact that mould growth has occurred does not necessarily mean that the food is unfit to eat. However, the presence of mould growth is usually a reliable indication that the food is old or has been stored in poor conditions. Moulds will grow on all types of food but they are particularly fond of meat, cheese and sweet foods. They grow best in a moist atmosphere at a temperature of 20–40°C. At lower temperatures moulds grow more slowly but growth can occur even at the temperature of a normal household refrigerator. Moulds grow

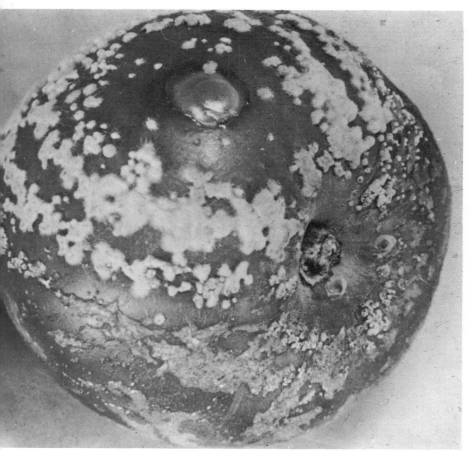

Mould colonies growing on a rotten apple

153

from tiny cells called spores which are carried in the atmosphere. When mould spores settle on food they infect it and if the mould grows the food will, of course, become mouldy. You can see colonies of mould growing on a rotten apple in the picture on page 153. Moulds and their spores are rapidly destroyed at the temperature of boiling water.

Yeasts. Yeasts are similar in many respects to moulds but they grow only on sugary foods. They consume the sugar and convert it to alcohol and in this way obtain the energy they need to grow and multiply. They grow best in roughly the same temperature range as moulds, and, like moulds, they grow more slowly at lower temperatures and can be destroyed by boiling water. Under favourable conditions they multiply with tremendous speed by budding, i.e. a small bud grows on the side of the yeast cell and when it has grown large enough it splits off and forms a new cell (see photograph).

Bacteria. The third type of micro-organism which causes food spoilage is the bacterium. Bacteria multiply very rapidly in warm moist conditions and thousands of millions of bacteria can arise from one individual in the space of a few days. They can be destroyed by heating but are more difficult to kill than moulds and yeasts. Some types are more resistant to heat than others, and the nature of the food in which they are found also influences the ease with which bacteria can be killed by heating. In acidic foods, such as fruits, bacteria die rapidly at the temperature of boiling water but in non-acid foods, such as vegetables and meat, they can withstand much higher temperatures.

Micro-organisms are present in water, dust, soil, sewage and on the hands of workers. As a result their presence in food is more-or-less inevitable. They are not all harmful, however, and some of the most prized food flavours in cheeses and fermented foods (such as yoghourt) are the result of the growth of micro-organisms. On the other hand, some *are* harmful and their presence in food may cause *food poisoning* (see Chapter 9). If food is to be kept in its original condition for any length of time it is essential that the growth of micro-organisms is prevented as far as possible. This can be done either by killing the micro-organisms and preventing further attack, or by proper storage.

154

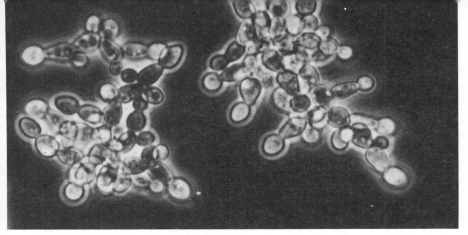

These three photographs show what micro-organisms look like when highly magnified.
Top. Highly magnified yeast cells multiplying by budding
Middle. Mould, magnified 50 times
Bottom. Food bacterium, magnified 5000 times

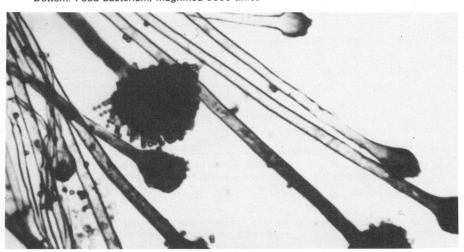

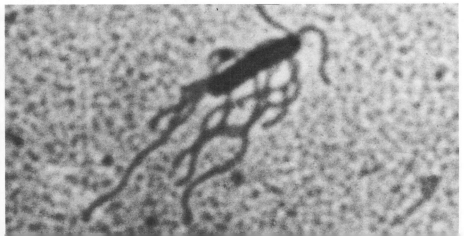

★ ? What are the three types of micro-organism that cause food to go bad? Under what conditions do they multiply rapidly?

PRESERVING FOOD

Butter, cheese, margarine; we have discussed all these earlier and they are all examples of convenience foods. Butter and cheese were originally made to use surplus milk which would otherwise go bad; in this sense they are preserved forms of milk. Margarine too is a form of preserved milk. In all these cases the milk has been processed so that the food may be stored for considerable periods; in addition they are convenience foods in the sense that they can be used as they are; no further preparation or cooking is necessary.

★ ? Apart from butter, cheese and margarine what other convenience or preserved forms of milk can you think of?

The table below summarizes the main ways in which food is preserved.

METHODS OF PRESERVING FOOD

Method	Principle	Examples
1. Chemical preservatives	Preservatives kill micro-organisms and prevent further attack	Vinegar (pickles and sauces). Sulphur dioxide (jam, sausages)
2. Dehydration	Without water micro-organisms cannot grow or multiply	Dried food and Freeze dried food (vegetables, fish, meat)
3. Canning, bottling	Heat kills micro-organisms. Food is in a sealed container and cannot be reinfected	Canned and bottled food (vegetables, meat, etc.)
4. Freezing	At very low temperatures micro-organisms are either killed or growth is prevented	Frozen and quick frozen food (vegetables, meat, etc.)

156

Preservatives

★★★ **Keypoint.** The micro-organisms in a food can be killed by treatment with a chemical which poisons them. If sufficient of the chemical is left in the food it will act as a preservative and prevent further attack by micro-organisms.

This is the basis of preservation by smoking, which has been used for preserving fish and meat for many centuries. The food is hung in the smoke from burning wood, and chemicals in the wood-smoke kill any micro-organisms on the food and help to prevent further attack.

Many chemicals are known which will poison micro-organisms, but unfortunately most of them are poisonous to human beings as well and so are unsuitable for use in foods. Substances which are harmful to man may not be used as preservatives.

At the present time only a handful of chemicals, known as *permitted preservatives*, may be added to food to preserve it. One of these is the choking gas sulphur dioxide which is used in sausages and soft drinks among other foods. The maximum amount that can be used varies from food to food, but in no case does it exceed three parts per thousand parts of the food. Some people can taste extremely small amounts of sulphur dioxide, but when foods containing it are cooked most of it is driven off. Even the permitted preservatives may only be used in certain foods. These are mainly bottled goods such as pickles, sauces, fruit juices and soft drinks. Such foods are not eaten at one sitting but may be in use over a period of time and the preservative prevents attack by micro-organisms during this period.

★ ? What products can you think of that are preserved in vinegar?

Dehydration

★★★ **Keypoint.** Micro-organisms, like all other living things, cannot grow and reproduce without water. If the water content of a food is reduced to below a certain level micro-organisms will not flourish in it.

Not all the water need be removed from a food to make it unattractive to micro-organisms. Jam, for example, contains about 25% water but it can be kept for long periods without harm.

157

This is because it also contains about 70% of sugar which dissolves in the water and makes it unavailable to micro-organisms. In fact, when micro-organisms are placed in contact with such concentrated solutions, water is absorbed from them and they die. If jam is made incorrectly so that it contains too little sugar it may easily go mouldy.

Condensation of water on the surface of jam may also reduce the sugar concentration at this point to such an extent that spots of mould may appear. The bulk of the jam is unaffected, however, and may be safely eaten after the mould has been skimmed off. Condensed sweetened milk stays wholesome for a considerable period after the tin is opened for the same reason; namely that the concentration of sugar is so high. The preservation of meat and vegetables by salting also depends on the fact that the salt dissolves in the water to form a more concentrated solution than can be tolerated by micro-organisms.

Water can be removed from food by drying it in the sun and this method is still used in some countries for drying fish and fruit such as grapes and plums. Methods of drying food using high temperatures have led in the past to inferior products and for this reason dried foods, such as dried vegetables, gained a poor reputation. New methods of drying, involving rapid drying at low temperature, have recently been developed and have been responsible for a great improvement in quality. The advent of quick-dried 'Surprise' peas, for example, gave dried peas a completely new image and the small time required to hydrate and cook them means that they are ideal convenience foods.

One of the most recent methods for preserving food is a new method of drying known as *freeze-drying*. As the name implies this involves drying food which has previously been frozen. It may seem strange that frozen food can be dried at all, but even frozen washing on a clothes line will dry if it is given enough time. This is because ice can be converted directly into water vapour without passing through an intermediate liquid stage. Although drying by this method is very slow at normal atmospheric pressure it can be speeded up tremendously by reducing the pressure and by heating, and this is what is done in the freeze-drying of food. Freeze-drying is a relatively expensive method of preservation, but because of its advantages a wide variety of foods is now preserved using this technique.

In most methods of dehydration the food must be sliced or

158

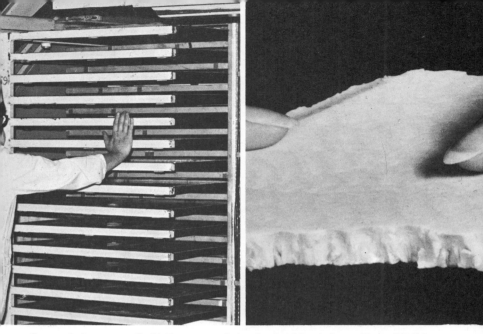

Freeze drying eggs—(Left) Frozen egg being loaded into drying cabinet. (Right) Freeze dried egg is light and brittle

minced to present the maximum possible surface area to the hot air current which carries away the moisture. In freeze-drying, however, large pieces of food, such as complete steaks, can be dried whole. Moreover the food is dried without destroying its structure, so that fragile foods such as prawns and shrimps can be freeze-dried intact. The introduction of dishes, such as prawn curries and chicken supreme, in an instant form owes much to the development of freeze-drying. These quite popular convenience foods consist largely of dried and freeze-dried items in which nearly all the preparation required is carried out in the factory leaving the housewife with nothing to do except rehydrate and heat the contents of various packets.

★★★ **Keypoint.** The great advantage of dehydrated food is its lightness and compactness compared with fresh food. This is especially true for foods like potatoes which contain large amounts of water. The powder obtained by dehydrating one ton of potatoes occupies only eight cubic feet and so it can be packed into a box only two foot square! This means that dehydrated foods are easily transported and so are especially valuable for emergency use in feeding large numbers of people.

159

★★ Activity. Visit a supermarket and see if you can find samples of the following preserved by freeze-drying (AFD):

coffee, peas and ingredients of complete dishes (e.g. Vesta). How long do the peas take to cook and how does this compare with fresh peas?

Canning

★★★ Keypoint. Micro-organisms in food can be killed by heating. If the food is heated in a closed container, such as a glass jar or metal can, micro-organisms are unable to get at it to re-infect it. This is the basis of preservation by bottling and canning.

If you want a good symbol for convenience foods you can't do better than choose the *can*. Nowadays millions of tons of every sort of food you can think of are canned every year. Everything that is from beans to beer to baby foods and from instant puddings to imitation meat. Not only are individual foods canned but complete meals in a can are now available which only need to be heated through to provide an instant meal.

Cans—an abbreviation of the word canister—are made from sheet steel coated with a very thin layer of tin. The tin coating is extremely thin and its purpose is to prevent the steel from corroding. Although the containers are often called 'tins' it should be remembered that their tin content is very small. For some foods the inside surface of the can is lacquered with a special varnish which prevents blackening of the tin coating.

Food intended for canning is carefully cleaned and, where necessary, peeled. Fruit and vegetables may be 'blanched' by boiling water or steam to soften them, to make it easier to pack them into the can and to destroy enzymes. The prepared food is placed in cans which are then filled with hot liquid. Sugar syrup is used for fruits and salt water for vegetables. The cans are heated almost to the boiling point of water to expel air and the lid is then sealed on. The can is now ready for heat-sterilization or 'processing' as it is called. The temperature to which it is heated depends upon the kind of food in the can, and the time for which it is heated upon the size of the can. Acid foods such as fruit need only be heated to the boiling point of water but non-acid foods such as meat are processed at 115°C. The heating period lasts for 10–30 minutes

160

for fruits and 25–50 minutes for vegetables. Large cans are heated for a longer period than small ones because of the extra time needed for the heat to penetrate to the middle of the food.

Canned foods will keep for long periods if the cans are not opened. Recently some very old cans of food were opened and the contents examined. The plum pudding in a tin sealed in 1900 was found to be in excellent condition. Meat canned in 1823 was found to be free from attack by micro-organisms, but the fat had partly broken down into glycerol and fatty acids. A number of fifty-year-old cans which had been taken on Antarctic expeditions by Scott and Shackleton and brought back unopened, were also found to be perfectly wholesome.

Nutritive value of canned foods. Some nutrient loss occurs during canning and more vitamin B_1 may be lost from meat during processing than would be lost during normal cooking. Reduction in vitamin C content also occurs during processing but much more disappears during the first few weeks of storage as a result of oxidation by the small amount of oxygen remaining in the top of the can. Further destruction of vitamin B_1 may occur during

Canning peas—Hot peas and boiling brine are filled into cans (right) which are sealed (left) before sterilizing

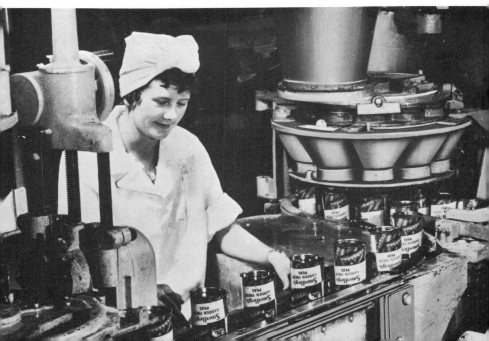

Vegetables to be frozen usually require a preliminary blanching with boiling water in order to inactivate enzymes. Blanching preserves colour, flavour and nutritional value; without blanching vitamin C is rapidly destroyed and unpleasant flavours are produced. Blanching time varies for different vegetables and needs to be carefully controlled — it needs to be long enough to inactivate the enzymes but not long enough to cook the vegetable. After blanching vegetables should be cooled as quickly as possible

storage but in normal conditions this should not exceed 10–15% during two years storage.

Apart from the losses of the two vitamins mentioned above canned foods are quite as good, from a nutritional point of view, as corresponding fresh foods. Indeed, canned fruits and vegetables may be better because they are often canned within a few hours of being picked and this reduces pre-canning losses of vitamin C to a minimum. The total loss of vitamin C in canned fruit and vegetables may be much less than in 'fresh' vegetables bought in a semi-fresh condition and cooked at home.

★ ? What are the main advantages of canned foods? What foods can you think of that cannot be canned successfully?

★★ **Activity.** Note the price of six fruits and vegetables available in your local shops. Can you find them canned in a supermarket? How do the prices per unit weight compare?

Frozen food

Sales of frozen foods are increasing more rapidly than those of any other convenience food. During the last 20 years the number of U.K. homes owning a freezer has increased very rapidly and frozen foods are no longer the novelty they were during the Sixties. They make seasonal produce available all the year, they can be frozen when they are in their prime condition and they remain in this condition as long as they remain frozen. In addition they are excellent convenience foods giving complete elimination of waste, rapid cooking and simple meal preparation. Moreover the range of foods that can be frozen is very large and new products are constantly being developed. A whole range of desserts, including ice-cream products and mousses, can be marketed only as frozen foods. So many convenience foods are now available in frozen form that whole sections of supermarkets are devoted to them (see photo below).

★★★ **Keypoint.** The basic principle of preservation by freezing is that micro-organisms multiply much more slowly at low temperatures than at normal air temperatures; and that enzyme activity almost ceases.

The range of frozen foods now available is so large that whole sections of supermarkets are devoted to them

Refrigeration. Food that is to be stored for short periods may be chilled, and this is the principle of the domestic refrigerator which operates at about 5°C. Commercially lower temperatures are used. For example, meat chilled to about −1°C will remain in good condition for up to one month.

The water present in chilled food is not frozen despite the temperature of −1°C, because dissolved solids present in the water lower its freezing point. At temperatures below −10°C, however, the water present in most foods is frozen and such foods can be safely kept for quite long periods. Use is made of this fact in transporting meat from Australia and New Zealand to this country. The meat is kept at −10°C or below both on the ship and after arrival in this country.

Freezing. Chilling to 5°C or below enables food to be stored for short periods but if it is to be stored for a longer time it must be frozen and stored at considerably lower temperatures. If the storage temperature is lowered to −10°C micro-organisms, which are the main causes of food spoilage, become inactive. However if enzyme activity, which causes loss of quality (colour, flavour and smell), is to be prevented the temperature must be lowered to at least −18°C. In practice home freezers store food at about −18°C and commercial freezers operate at about −29°C. This latter temperature is low enough to ensure a long storage life and high quality.

The *rate* at which foods are frozen is important because only if the freezing is quick can good quality be obtained. This can be understood from Fig. 41. During fast freezing tiny ice crystals are formed within the *vacuoles* of the cells and because they do not have time to grow they do not distort the structure of the cell. On the other hand, if freezing occurs slowly ice crystals start to form *outside* the vacuole in the spaces between the cells. As these crystals grow they draw water from within the cells leaving them distorted. Some crystals may also form within the vacuoles.

When food that has been frozen slowly is thawed its structure is spoilt and its texture will be poor. Considerable 'drip' or loss of liquid may occur. There may also be some loss of food value. For example fruit, particularly soft fruit such as strawberries, lose much liquid on thawing out and suffer from partial collapse of their cell structure. Also there is loss of vitamin C contained in the drip.

164

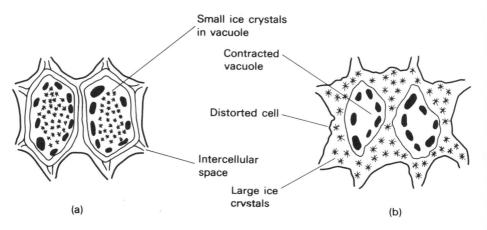

Fig. 41. Formation of ice crystals in food : (a) the small crystals which result from quick freezing and (b) the large crystals and distorted cells resulting from slow freezing

Foods are quick-frozen either by the traditional method of cooling them between cooled plates or by the more recent fluidized technique in which cold air is blown up through the food producing what is known as a fluidized bed. This method is especially useful for quick-freezing small, regular-shaped vegetables such as peas and diced carrots which are kept in motion in the cold air rather like table tennis balls bouncing on a table (see picture below). This process produces a free-flowing product that can be

Quick-freezing of peas which are seen moving through a freezer tunnel

sold in 'pour and store' packs that are convenient to the consumer who can buy large economic quantities, pour out the exact amount required and store the rest in the freezer compartment of a refrigerator.

The newest method of freezing is known as *cryogenic freezing*; it involves the use of very low boiling liquids such as liquid nitrogen in which the food is immersed. Alternatively these extremely cold liquids may be sprayed on to the food, but whichever method is used the freezing is extremely rapid and foods frozen in this way retain their original shape and appearance. Some luxury foods such as strawberries, shrimps and scampi are being frozen by this new method.

Nutritive value of frozen foods. Quick freezing is one of the safest and most efficient methods of food preservation. Quick-frozen foods resemble fresh foods more closely and retain a higher proportion of their original nutritive value than foods preserved by any other process except freeze drying.

The food value of frozen food may well be *higher* than that of so-called 'fresh' food which, in the case of vegetables, may have been picked a week or more before they are cooked. Peas for freezing are frozen and packed 90 minutes after being harvested; quite an achievement! Frozen vegetables, such as peas, and frozen fruits, such as blackcurrants, are likely to contain more vitamin C than when 'fresh'.

★★ **Activity.** Buying peas.

HOW WE BUY PEAS

Type	% of total bought
Quick-frozen	35
Canned garden	20
Canned processed	25
Fresh and others	20

Find samples of each type of pea mentioned in the table above and compare their relative costs. Which is the best value for money and why? Compare the advantages of frozen peas and fresh peas.

Processed food and additives

Potato crisps, breakfast cereals, instant puddings and instant coffee; these are typical convenience foods, but they are more than preserved forms of fresh foods—they have been *processed* in some way. In essence processing is mainly cooking performed on a large scale and it involves such operations as mixing, heating and cooling. It also involves the treatment of raw materials such as the threshing and milling of grain and the extraction of sucrose from sugar beet and sugar cane discussed earlier. Unlike home cooking, processing involves also the use of additives, i.e. the addition of small amounts of substances such as nutrients, preservatives or flavours.

'What is the purpose of processing?' You may well ask. Well, it 'improves' the food by making it more convenient and more attractive. It may improve colour, texture and flavour (see Chapter 12); it may improve keeping properties or nutritional value; it may reduce the need for preparation and cooking.

Let us take the example of starch to illustrate what we mean. Ordinary wheat starch is not in convenience form because it does not dissolve in cold water but when a mixture of starch and water is heated a big change in texture occurs for the starch granules swell greatly and gelatinize producing a very thick jelly-like material—the familiar starch paste. Thus starch is widely used in products which are designed to thicken on cooking; sauces, dried soup powders and canned soups are familiar examples of convenience foods that use starch as a thickening agent.

Although ordinary starch cannot be used to thicken instant foods which are prepared without cooking, its properties are changed considerably when it is processed by being heated and dried. Such pre-cooked starch rapidly forms a thick paste when mixed with cold water and in this form starch forms the basic ingredient of an *instant pudding* providing both its bulk and its smooth, solid consistency. Apart from pre-cooked starch an instant pudding such as Instant Whip contains sugar, salt, flavours, colours and sodium phosphate. Each of the ingredients present has a definite function; colours are added to make the product look attractive, flavours to make it taste good while sodium phosphate is needed to coagulate milk proteins and thus make the pudding set when milk is added to the powder, just as egg-white sets or coagulates when an egg is heated.

167

Food Additives. As time goes by we are eating more and more convenience foods—and that means we are eating more and more additives. Additives are chemicals that are added to food to ' improve ' it in some way. We have already seen that chemicals may be added to food to preserve it—but additives have many other uses. They are used to modify colour, flavour and texture; to improve the keeping qualities of food and to make processing easier. They are used to control moisture and acidity and they are used to improve nutritional value.

Thousands of different substances are now used as additives. The largest group of additives are flavours of which there are over one thousand in use. To some people the increasing number of additives being used is a cause for concern, if not alarm, and it is important to emphasise that the use of additives is most carefully controlled. Regulations govern what additives may be used, the amounts that may be used and the foods to which they may be added. The safety of additives is tested most carefully before their use is permitted in food.

★ ? The following is a description of a convenience food as listed on the back of the pack; sugar, vegetable oil (with antioxidant), corn starch, sodium caseinate, emulsifier, sodium phosphate, flavour, lecithin, lactose, colour. Can you work out what the product is? It is an instant whip dessert. Note that ingredients are always listed in order of importance—so that sugar is the main, and colour the least ingredient.

Value for money

It is important that we can assess convenience foods properly, and decide if we are getting value for money. Here are the factors that we must consider:

1. Saving of time. Convenience foods can often be eaten straight out of the packet or can, others require only heating up. On the other hand some convenience foods do not save time. For example, if you buy a pancake batter mix you need to add water to the powdered mix and beat well. In making a home made batter you simply beat together flour, milk and an egg. So here the only time and effort saved by using the packet mix is that of measuring the flour and breaking the egg!

168

2. *Saving in cost of cooking.* Cost of gas or electricity for cooking may be reduced. Compare a canned stew with a fresh stew from this point of view.

3. *Total cost.* Convenience foods nearly always cost more than the corresponding fresh food. In comparing costs remember that some convenience foods require the addition of extra ingredients—such as milk or an egg—and the cost of these must be included.

4. *Nutritive value.* This needs careful consideration. Frozen peas have a nutritive value at least as high as that of fresh foods. The food value of instant coffee is nil—but so is that of coffee beans! The food value of instant pudding mix is probably low (mainly carbohydrate), but when it is prepared milk is added, and this gives it a food value similar to that of a rice pudding, for example.

5. *Appearance.* Convenience foods are often attractive. If an instant pudding is attractive it may be eaten whereas a rice pudding might not be. They can both be regarded nutritionally as forms of milk.

6. *Palatability.* Compare the flavour and general palatability of the fresh and convenience product.

★★ **Activity.** Buy an instant pudding, a cake mix and a ready-to-eat dinner and compare them with the equivalent home-made product in terms of the six factors listed above.

★★ **Activity.** Look at a selection of breakfast cereal packets and note what nutrients have been added to them. What do you think about their food value? Compare the food value of the cereals with the milk that is added to them when they are eaten. Compare bread and cereals (both convenience foods) using the six points given above.

★★★ **Keypoint.** Note one disadvantage of supermarkets and convenience foods. The way that food is displayed—its attractive package, its prominent position to catch your eye, its 'special' price—may tempt you to buy a luxury food of small food value instead of a more basic but less glamorous product with a higher food value.

169

9 Food and Hygiene

It is useless to plan a carefully balanced diet and produce well cooked meals, if when we eat we suffer from stomach pains or other ill-effects. We must always take the greatest possible care to see that the food we eat is as clean and safe as it can be.

Food poisoning

If we eat food that has gone bad or been infected in some way we may suffer from *food poisoning*. We saw in the last chapter that the air we breathe, the things we touch and the food we eat all contain minute organisms called *bacteria*. We noted that although many types of bacteria are harmless, there are some that are definitely harmful. It is these disease-producing or *pathogenic* bacteria that cause food poisoning.

We cannot prevent *some* harmful bacteria entering our bodies, but we must ensure that their numbers are kept small. If this is so, they will have little or no effect on us. It is only when our systems are invaded by large numbers of pathogenic bacteria that we suffer from food poisoning. Bacteria multiply so rapidly in favourable conditions (for example warmth and moisture) that thousands of millions of bacteria may arise from a single bacterium in only a few days. It is obvious therefore that food must be stored and prepared in conditions that are unfavourable to bacterial growth.

★★★ **Keypoint.** Most food poisoning in Britain is caused by the *Salmonella* group of bacteria. These poisonous bacteria cause diarrhoea, stomach pains, sickness and, in severe cases, death.

Salmonella bacteria are mainly spread by infected people who handle food—especially if they touch food with unwashed hands after using the toilet (see photo on page 171). The droppings of infected mice and rats, food—such as milk, meat and manu-

170

factured meat products—from infected animals, also lead to food poisoning from Salmonella bacteria.

Food poisoning may also be caused by bacteria which produce their poison in the food. The *Staphylococcus* group of bacteria act in this way. The effects of such poisoning are rather like bad seasickness and include sickness and extreme weakness. These bacteria are mainly spread from the nose and mouth (by coughs and sneezes) and from cuts and scratches on the hands of infected people who handle food.

Infection from *Staphylococcal* bacteria will only cause food poisoning if the poison is given time to form. This can be prevented by cooking food thoroughly immediately after preparation. It should also be cooled rapidly after it has been cooked. If infected food is allowed to stand in warm moist conditions for any length of time, the bacteria multiply and poison is formed. The poison is rather resistant to heat treatment and subsequent cooking may fail to destroy it once it is formed.

Food which is cooked and then stored for some time in warm moist conditions may cause food poisoning even though cooking has destroyed all the bacteria. This is explained by the fact that when some bacteria find themselves in conditions which do not favour growth, they develop *spores* which are resistant to heat. The spores therefore survive cooking and if such food is stored in warm moist conditions the spores go back to their active form and multiply rapidly. Thus if such food—especially cooked meat products—is badly stored it can easily cause food poisoning.

Clostridium perfringens causes food poisoning of this type which often occurs in canteens and other large-scale catering units where meat is cooked before it is required, is allowed to cool and is then reheated before serving.

★ ? Once food has been cooked why is it important either to eat it at once or cool it rapidly and keep it covered in a cool place?

★★★ **Keypoint.** Food that may have been contaminated with Salmonellae must be cooked really well to destroy any such bacteria present.

★★★ **Keypoint.** Most food poisoning (at least 80%) in Britain is caused by meat and poultry products.

171

BACTERIA CAUSING FOOD POISONING

Organisms involved	Foods commonly affected	Illness		Comment
		Incubation period	Duration	
Salmonellae	Meat, especially sliced cooked meat and meat pies. Duck eggs. Synthetic cream. Ice-cream. Shellfish	12–36 hours	1–8 days	Main cause of food poisoning in U.K. Unpleasant, often with severe diarrhoea but not usually serious
Clostridium perfringens	Gravy, stews, pre-cooked meat	8–22 hours	12–24 hours	Can occur when food is kept hot. Causes severe stomach pains
Staphylococci	Pies, meat, especially sliced meats, pies and gravy. Synthetic cream. Ice-cream	2–6 hours	6–24 hours	Unpleasant but not normally serious. Causes severe vomiting
Clostridium botulinum	Inadequately processed canned meat, vegetables and fish	24–72 hours	Often death within a week	Very rare but often fatal
Bacillus cereus	Rice, cornflour, meat products	2–15 hours	6–24 hours	Fairly common. Causes severe vomiting, stomach pains and diarrhoea

Food poisoning in Britain is on the increase and more cases are reported every year. There are many reasons for this. For example, there has been an *increase in large-scale catering* and this means that a single infected food can produce many cases of food poisoning. There has also been an *increase in factory farming* of poultry and other animals and this increases the possibility of large-scale infection of food, especially with Salmonella.

There has been an *increase in the staff untrained in hygiene* in large-scale catering. This means that *cross-contamination*, which is the transfer of bacteria from a contaminated source, such as a knife, to uncontaminated food, can easily occur and spread infection.

There has been an *increase in take-away meals* and fast-food outlets where food may be kept warm for long periods and briefly reheated before eating so allowing rapid growth of bacteria.

★★★ **Keypoint.** To prevent further increase in food poisoning there needs to be more education to make people aware of the dangers and also to improve standards of hygiene.

★ ? The shells of hen eggs (and duck eggs) are often infected with Salmonella and cause infection of commercial liquid egg. Why do you think that all bulk liquid egg must be pasteurised?

Personal hygiene

Pathogenic bacteria are found both inside the body and on its surface, and such bacteria may be transferred to food by people who handle it if precautions are not taken. Infection may be spread in this way both in factories during food manufacture, and during preparation and cooking of food in restaurants, canteens and homes.

★★★ **Keypoint.** It cannot be urged too strongly that personal hygiene is of the greatest importance at *all* times, and *especially* when handling food.

173

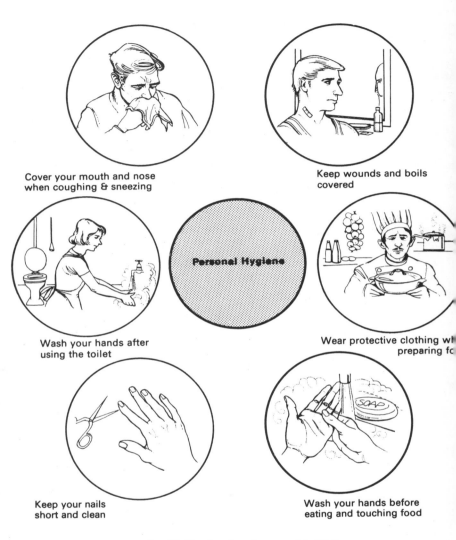

Cover your mouth and nose when coughing & sneezing

Keep wounds and boils covered

Personal Hygiene

Wash your hands after using the toilet

Wear protective clothing wh preparing fo

Keep your nails short and clean

Wash your hands before eating and touching food

Fig. 42. Simple rules of personal hygiene

Bacteria from the bowels find their way onto the hands during use of the toilet (see page 186), and it is therefore essential to wash the hands properly afterwards. Food handlers should keep their finger nails short and clean, and wash their hands before touching food. Everyone should wash their hands before eating a meal.

174

It is true that 'coughs and sneezes spread diseases' and when coughing or sneezing the mouth and nose should be covered with a clean handkerchief.

Cuts, scratches, pimples, boils, etc., collect bacteria and should always be covered with a waterproof dressing. It is also good practice for food handlers to wear clean protective clothing to cover both the body and the hair. Such clothing should be washed frequently.

★ ? It is most important that these simple rules of personal hygiene should be carried out. Look at Fig. 42; do you always carry them out as a matter of normal routine?

★★ **Activity.** Make up an Agar jelly (or one made with a stock cube and gelatin—about 30 g to $\frac{1}{2}$ litre of water). Pour the liquid into six petri dishes that have been carefully cleaned and cover (or use glass baby-food jars). Allow to set. Use the petri dishes as follows:

1. Leave covered as a control. 2. Cough onto jelly surface. 3. Impress washed fingers onto the jelly. 4. Impress unwashed fingers onto the jelly after using the toilet. 5. Put several human hairs onto the jelly. 6. Impress unwashed dishcloth onto the surface.

Cover all the dishes and leave in a warm place (30–40°C) for 3–4 days. How do you explain the results?

HYGIENE IN THE KITCHEN

Personal hygiene is most important, but by itself it is not enough. *Every* aspect of food storage, handling and preparation must be carried out in a hygienic way. It only needs *one* weak link in a chain to make the chain snap. In a similar way it only needs *one* stage of food preparation to be unhygienic for the chance of infection to occur (Fig. 43).

There is more activity in the kitchen than in any other part of the house, and as the housewife does the greater part of her work there, it is important that the kitchen should be pleasant, efficient and clean. Otherwise—if, for example, the lighting is bad, the floor uneven or the sink the wrong height—the work done there will suffer. In order to keep the kitchen clean, all wall, floor and

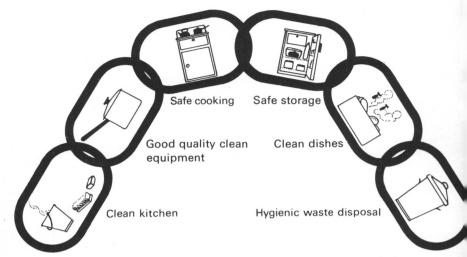

Fig. 43. Aspects of kitchen hygiene—essential links in the chain

working surfaces should be smooth without any cracks or other places where dirt or insects can lodge.

★★★ **Keypoint.** A *clean* kitchen is a *hygienic* one. It can only remain so if *all* the aspects of hygiene shown in the diagram above are attended to.

Kitchens should be designed with safety, hygiene and ease of use in mind. Walls covered with tiles, working surfaces of hard plastic and smooth thermoplastic flooring are all attractive, practical and easily kept clean.

Working surfaces should be washed down after using them for the preparation of food. Floors should be kept covered with a film of non-slip polish as this will prevent grease and dirt from becoming engrained in the surface. The polished surface is easily kept clean and shining with an occasional wipe over. Walls, ceiling and lights should be cleaned thoroughly as they have to withstand both grease and steam, and also fumes from the cooker.

When washing these kitchen surfaces a hot detergent solution should be used, and it is a good plan to add a little disinfectant to the water, so that bacteria are killed.

All equipment used in the kitchen must be kept spotlessly clean and should be well designed to make cleaning easy.

176

An old kitchen that has been redesigned for ease of working and cleaning

★★★ **Keypoint.** Remember that micro-organisms lodge in the inside corners of pans and in all crevices, cracks and other places that cannot be cleaned (e.g. between the prongs of a badly designed fork).

★★ **Activity.** Look at the picture above and list all the features that enable the kitchen to be kept clean easily.

The storage of food

If food is stored in warm moist conditions, bacterial growth will be encouraged and the food will soon become tainted. Food should therefore be stored in a cool dry atmosphere. Larders should be designed so that these necessary cool dry conditions are easily maintained. Plenty of ventilation should be provided; windows should face north and be fitted with fly-proof gauze. All parts of the larder should be cleaned frequently and strong-smelling foods should be kept in covered containers, so that the flavour of other stored foods is not spoilt.

Refrigerators. In winter even perishable foods, such as milk and meat, can safely be kept for a day in a larder. In summer, however, such foods deteriorate rapidly and are best kept in a refrigerator. In Britain the percentage of homes having a refrigerator has almost doubled in the last 10 years and is now over 80%.

It is important to appreciate that the temperature of a refrigerator outside the freezer compartment is about 5°C. Such a temperature is sufficiently low to reduce the activity of bacteria but it does not kill them so that many foods start to spoil if kept at this temperature for more than a few days. At 5°C enzyme action in food slows but is not halted and so chemical changes continue resulting in gradual deterioration of flavour, colour and smell.

★★★ **Keypoint.** Typical storage times in a refrigerator are; uncooked meat, several days (except minced meat not more than 1 day); white fish, not more than 1 or 2 days; milk, 3 or 4 days; butter, 2–3 weeks; margarine, up to 6 weeks; hard cheese, 2 or 3 weeks.

THE OPERATION OF A REFRIGERATOR (see Fig. 44)

Principle	Practical result
1. *Evaporation.* In the freezer compartment the liquid refrigerant evaporates and absorbs heat from the food-storage compartment which is therefore cooled	Food is cooled to below freezing point in the freezer itself but up to 10°C in the least cold part
2. *Air circulation.* Cold air is heavier than warm air, so cold air falls and warm air rises	Air circulates; air is coldest below the freezer and least cold at the top away from the freezer
3. *Absorption of moisture.* Moving air absorbs moisture	Moisture removed from food is deposited on the surface of freezer as ice.

178

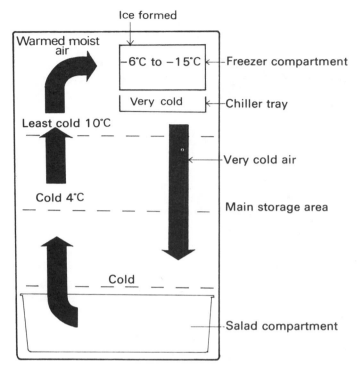

Fig. 44. Air circulation and variation of temperature inside a refrigerator

Modern refrigerators contain a freezer compartment in which frozen food can be kept frozen, for periods which vary according to the star-rating of the refrigerator. The details are given below.

THE STAR-RATING SYSTEM FOR FREEZER COMPARTMENTS AND FREEZERS

Rating	Maximum temperature	Period for which food can be kept frozen
* One	$-6°$	Up to one week
** Two	$-12°$	Up to one month
*** Three	$-18°$	Up to three months
**** Four	$-25°$ to $-30°$	At least three months

A fridge freezer showing the correct way to store food in the refrigerator compartment

THE USE OF A REFRIGERATOR (see photo)

Practical point	Reason
1. Most food in a refrigerator should be wrapped or put in a closed container	This prevents the food from drying out
2. Strong-smelling food such as cheese must be kept in closed air-tight containers	Other foods such as butter will absorb the odour
3. Food that easily perishes, e.g. meat, bacon, sausages, should be stored below the freezer (preferably in a chiller drawer)	The temperature is lowest here
4. Salad foods should be kept at the bottom in a covered 'crisper' compartment	Salad foods do not need to be kept very cold, but they should be covered to prevent loss of moisture (this causes lettuce to go 'flabby')
5. Bottles of milk and squash, fats, eggs and cans can be stored in the door compartment	They do not need to be stored at a very low temperature; fittings in the door make this a convenient place
6. A fridge should not be packed too full	Air cannot circulate freely and so the cooling effect is reduced
7. The door should be open for as little time as possible	Warm air from the kitchen gets in and raises the temperature
8. Hot food should not be put in, until it has cooled	It warms the air in the fridge

★★ **Activity.** Put a fresh banana in the salad compartment and another in the freezer. Inspect each day. Can all foods be stored successfully in a refrigerator?

★ ? How would you store the following in a refrigerator: cabbage, butter, kippers, bacon, tomatoes, eggs, a strong cheese, e.g. camembert?

181

Domestic freezers. If perishable foods are to be stored for a long period, temperatures below 5°C must be used. Domestic freezer cabinets store food at about − 18°C, and at these temperatures many perishable foods can be kept for up to a year.

★★★ **Keypoint.** Fresh food should only be frozen in freezers with a ★ ★★★ 4-star rating. In order to achieve good quality, food needs to be frozen quickly (see page 164). This can only be done by switching on the fast-freeze (super) switch 6 hours before adding the unfrozen food. This means that the temperature of the freezer will be about − 27°C when the unfrozen food is added.

Storing food in a freezer. Frozen food must be carefully packaged if it is to be stored in a freezer. There are several reasons for this;

1. *To prevent loss of moisture.* Uncovered frozen food dries out easily producing *freezer burn* which can be detected by whitish, discoloured patches on the surface of the food. Freezer burn is harmless but makes the food drier and tougher.
2. *To prevent rancidity.* Unsaturated fats (see page 26) and foods containing them, such as fried food and fatty meat and fish, react with oxygen in the air producing an unpleasant rancid taste and smell. Rancidity occurs only slowly at low temperatures and can be prevented by wrapping foods carefully to exclude air.
3. *To prevent transfer of strong smells.* Foods with a strong smell such as smoked meats, fish and cabbage must be carefully wrapped so that their strong smell is not transferred to other more delicately flavoured foods such as dairy products.
4. *To prevent enzyme action.* The colour, flavour, texture and vitamin C content of vegetables deteriorates unless they are *blanched* (see page 162) before freezing.

Suitable packaging material for frozen food include: heavy duty polythene bags or sheets, aluminium foil or dishes, rigid plastic boxes. The food must be completely covered by the packaging material, air must be removed and the package sealed.

Safe cooking

It is best to cook perishable food when it is as fresh as possible, though often some storage cannot be avoided. Once out of storage, food should be cooked at once.

Food should be cooked thoroughly so that it is cooked all through and not just at the surface. This applies especially to manufactured meat dishes, such as sausages, meat pies and rissoles. For such foods, which are liable to infection if not manufactured and stored under hygienic conditions, cooking must be sufficient to kill most bacteria.

After cooking, food which is not to be eaten hot, should be cooled rapidly and not allowed to stand in a warm kitchen.

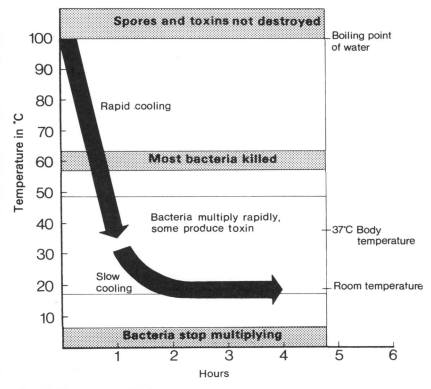

Fig. 45. The rate at which food cools showing how it remains in the danger zone (where bacteria multiply rapidly) for a long period

Warmth and moisture encourage bacterial growth, and although active bacteria may have been killed during cooking, heat resistant spores may become active and start multiplying. Food may also become reinfected with more bacteria.

★★★ **Keypoint.** It is dangerous to cool food slowly in the open kitchen. Fig. 45 makes this clear.

★ ? Under what conditions do bacteria multiply most rapidly?

★ ?Once food has become contaminated with bacteria does putting it into (a) boiling water and (b) a refrigerator always destroy the contamination?

If food cannot be eaten immediately after it has been cooked it should be stored in a cool larder or refrigerator. Foods such as gravy, soup and stock are ideal for bacterial growth and should not be stored.

If food is to be re-cooked after storage special care is necessary. This is because poison which is resistant to heat may develop during storage. In summer months cooked meat dishes, such as stews, pies and mince, are particularly liable to infection in this way. If such dishes are re-cooked, they should never be merely warmed through as this will fail to destroy the poison. They must be heated to a high temperature, and cooking must be continued until heat has penetrated right through the food.

A case history: an unfortunate lunch

The lunch. Twenty people sat down to an attractive-looking lunch of cold chicken and ham with salad on a warm sunny day.

The result. Within three hours they were all in hospital suffering from severe vomiting and diarrhoea.

The method of food preparation. The chicken had been cooked the day before, cut up and stored overnight in a cool larder (not a refrigerator). In the morning of the lunch a can of ham was opened, and the ham was cut into slices and put onto plates with the portions of chicken. They were then left to stand for three hours.

The explanation. The nature of the food poisoning and the rapidity with which it occurred suggested *Staphylococcal* food poisoning. The

184

cook was examined and found to be suffering from a nose infection; the discharge from his nose contained the same type of *Staphylococcus* as caused the food poisoning. The bacteria from his nose contaminated the chicken and ham; these bacteria multiplied slowly overnight in the chicken and rapidly while the food was standing in a warm room for three hours.

★★★ Keypoints.
1. Never allow cooked food to cool slowly; always store it overnight in a refrigerator.
2. Never leave food standing in the open for long, especially in a warm room.
3. No one who has any sort of discharge should handle food.

A high standard of personal hygiene is essential in all those who handle food.

The kitchen sink

Although badly washed dishes may *look* clean, they may in fact be covered by a thin film of grease containing bacteria. It is important that dish-washing is carried out properly so that dishes not only look clean but *are* clean.

Before washing up, food remains should be scraped off plates and dishes. The dishes should then be put into a sink containing a hot detergent solution. It is also good practice to add a little disinfectant to the washing up water. After dishes, utensils and cutlery have been thoroughly washed, they should be rinsed in hot clean water.

★ ? Why is it more hygienic to allow washed dishes to dry in air rather than dry them with a cloth? If a cloth is used it must be boiled frequently in boiling detergent solution. Why is this?

Disposal of waste

After food has been prepared and eaten waste material remains. This waste must be disposed of in a hygienic way, otherwise it may become a source of infection. House refuse, such as rotting food, may become a breeding place for flies; sugary waste attracts wasps in summer and bacteria breed in sour milk.

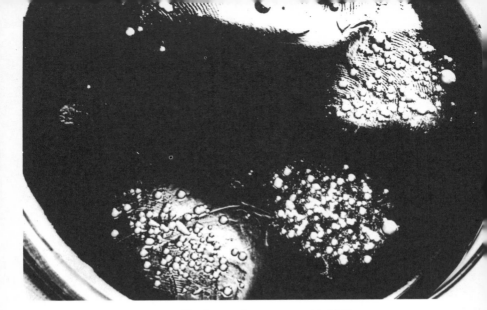

The danger of poor personal hygiene
A set of fingerprints obtained from an unwashed hand after using the toilet. The invisible bacteria on the hand have been allowed to grow on a nutrient jelly until they have developed into visible colonies

No solid waste material should be allowed to remain in the kitchen; it should be placed in a closed bin kept conveniently near the sink. Plastic containers with lids are suitable for this purpose. Such bins should be emptied and cleaned daily, and their contents transferred to a large bin, with a well fitting lid, kept outside. These bins should be emptied regularly, and after emptying they should be rinsed with a disinfectant solution. The area round the bin must also be kept clean.

Liquid waste may be poured down the sink, and the sink should then be rinsed with a solution of disinfectant. Milk bottles should be carefully rinsed and drained, and the inside of empty tins and jars washed out. If this is not done the food waste remaining in them is a possible source of infection.

★★ **Activity.** Look round your own kitchen at home. List the places where you might expect to find bacteria. How could the kitchen be improved from a hygiene point of view?

★ **?** What are the dangers of allowing food waste to remain in the kitchen? Why should empty milk bottles and jam jars be washed carefully?

186

10 Cooking I: Methods and Effects on Nutrients

Why do we eat some foods raw and others cooked? There are several reasons for this. Sometimes cooking improves the flavour of the food. For instance the flavour of uncooked flour or sour apples is not very pleasant, but when the flour has been converted into bread and the apples stewed with sugar, their flavour is much improved. On the other hand you would not cook fresh strawberries—this would spoil the delicious flavour of the raw fruit.

Cooking may also improve the attractiveness of food. You would not be very enthusiastic about eating a raw chop, but after cooking, it has an appetizing appearance and a good smell. Even more important, cooking may make a food more digestible. It would be difficult to eat the flesh of a raw chop (or uncooked flour) even if you wanted to, but after cooking, it is much more tender and so easier to chew and digest. Finally, cooking may improve the keeping quality of a food and make it safe. For example, milk may be boiled to delay the souring process and kill bacteria. The preservation of food by heat treatment is quite distinct from cooking, and was considered in Chapter 8.

★ ? Why is food cooked? List all the reasons you can think of.

★★★ **Keypoint.** Remember that cooking is only one part of food preparation. Apart from the actual cooking process, ingredients may have to be blended together and they may need special preparation by soaking, sieving or chopping and in other ways. Seasoning, spices, herbs, sauces may be used to improve the flavour; colour and garnishes may be added to improve attractiveness, texture may be improved by grinding, mashing, mixing and in other ways.

★★ Activity. Plan an attractive meal that involves plenty of food preparation but no cooking.

Methods of cooking

Cooked food is food that has been changed in various ways by heat treatment. The heat may be applied in a number of ways; it may be dry or moist, it may be applied by means of fat or by infrared radiation.

1. Dry-heat methods. Dry heat cooking may be done in an oven and when food is cooked in this way it is said to be *baked*. Baking is rather a slow method of cooking, but it has the advantage that large quantities of food can be cooked and the food is cooked evenly. Sometimes the food to be cooked is put into the oven in a tin containing a little fat; food cooked in this way is said to be *roasted*. Meat and potatoes are the foods most often cooked by roasting.

Cooking temperatures used in an oven vary from below 100°C (very slow) to about 260°C (very hot) as shown in Fig. 46.

Grilling is another method of applying dry heat. The food to be grilled is placed beneath a red-hot source of heat, usually a glowing metal grid. Radiant heat is directed onto the surface of the food which is rapidly heated. Grilling heat is applied to the top surface of the food and so the food should be turned from time to time. *Infra-red grilling* makes use of heat rays which have longer wavelengths than visible light. Some of the radiation used in normal grilling is of this kind, but in infra-red cookery the proportion of infra-red radiation is much increased, and this reduces cooking time to such an extent that a steak, for example, may be cooked in a minute.

Contact grills use infra-red radiation for making toasted sandwiches and for grilling steaks and chops rapidly. Heat is conveyed to the food by contact with the plates.

2. Moist heat methods. Although cooking with water involves using low temperatures, it is a relatively quick method of cooking because water has a big capacity for holding heat and for transferring this heat rapidly to food by means of convection (p. 192). In moist heat cooking food is heated either by water or steam. *Boiling* uses boiling water, *simmering* uses water near, but below

188

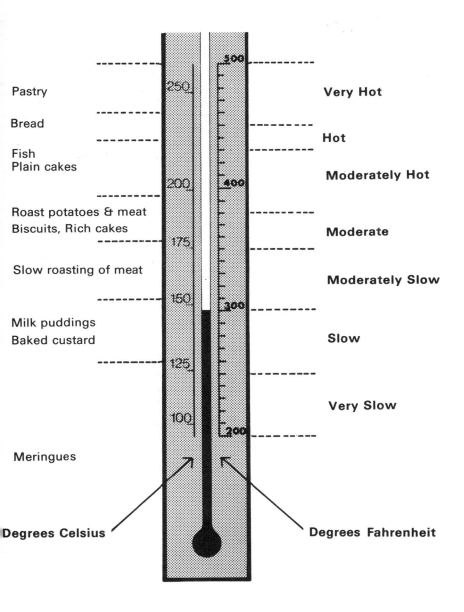

	Degrees Celsius	Degrees Fahrenheit	
Pastry	250	500	Very Hot
Bread			
			Hot
Fish			
Plain cakes	200	400	Moderately Hot
Roast potatoes & meat			
Biscuits, Rich cakes	175		Moderate
Slow roasting of meat			Moderately Slow
	150	300	
Milk puddings			
Baked custard			Slow
	125		
			Very Slow
	100	200	
Meringues			

Fig. 46. Oven temperatures

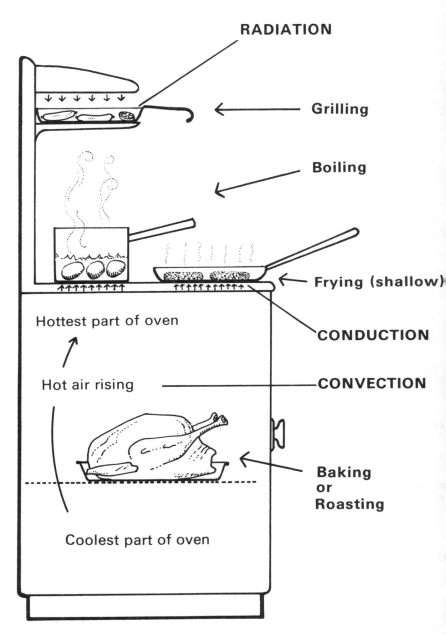

Fig. 47. Methods of cooking and ways in which heat is transferred to food

boiling point, and is similar to both *stewing* (for meat and fruit) and *poaching* (for fish).

'Boil in the bag' cooking uses boiling water indirectly, but because the food is sealed in the bag this method prevents loss of flavour and soluble nutrients into the cooking water. In *steaming*, steam is used directly to heat the food or indirectly to heat the container. Although steaming is slower than boiling, cooking may be speeded up by the use of a *pressure cooker*, in which steam is produced at higher than normal pressure. Increase of pressure raises the temperature at which water boils, so the cooking temperature is increased, and the cooking time reduced. For example, suet puddings may be cooked in about 50 minutes instead of the usual $2\frac{1}{2}$ hours, and tough cuts of meat may be cooked in about 15 minutes instead of at least 2 hours.

In essence a pressure cooker is a pan with a well-fitting lid arranged so that steam can be safely generated under pressure. The pan and lid lock together by means of a groove to make the cooker pressure-tight (Fig. 48). The food to be cooked and the required amount of water are put into the pan, which is then closed. When the closed pan is heated air is driven out through the air vent until the cooker is full of steam. In pressure cookers with a pressure indicator—as shown in the diagram—the vent then closes

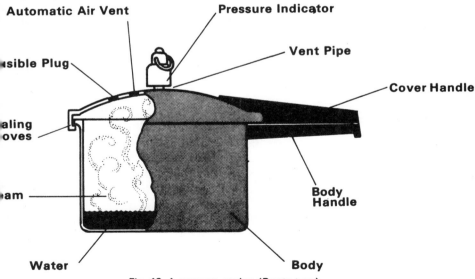

Automatic Air Vent   **Pressure Indicator**

Vent Pipe

isible Plug

Cover Handle

aling oves

am

Body Handle

Water   **Body**

Fig. 48. A pressure cooker (Presto type)

191

and pressure builds up to the value required. Slow heating only is then needed to maintain this pressure, which is shown by the pressure indicator. Should the pressure rise too much, steam automatically escapes through the air vent. The fusible plug is a second safety device; this melts if the cooker overheats or boils dry.

3. Frying. In *frying*, food is cooked in hot fat. Fat has a very much higher boiling point than water and can be heated almost to its boiling point without smoking. Frying is a quick method of cooking because of the high temperature that is used. In *shallow frying*, a shallow pan is used and enough fat is added to cover the bottom of the pan. Although such a method is quick, heating of the food is uneven and it should be turned from time to time. Lard, dripping and vegetable oils (such as olive oil, corn oil and cottonseed oil often blended together) are best for shallow frying. In *deep frying*, a deep pan and plenty of fat are used, so that when the food is added it is completely covered by the fat, which should be very hot. Temperatures of between 150°C and 200°C are usually used, and the temperature of the fat may be checked with a thermometer. Such a method is quick and the food is cooked evenly on all sides. Refined vegetable oils or cooking fats—which are made by hardening a blend of vegetable, animal and marine oil—are best for deep frying.

Ways in which heat is transferred

In cooking heat from the cooker is transferred to food by conduction, by convection and by radiation. These three methods are illustrated in Fig. 47 and summarized below.

1. Conduction. Heat flows through materials from hot areas to cooler ones. Some materials such as metals are good conductors and allow heat to pass through them easily. This is why cooking pans are made of metals (except for the handles which are made of bad conductors; why is this?). In Fig. 47 heat from the cooker heats up the frying pan by conduction. Heat is transferred from the hot pan to the cooler fat and as this heats up heat is passed to the cold food by conduction.

2. Convection. Hot gases and liquids rise, cold ones sink. Thus in an oven, for example (see Fig. 47) hot air rises and cold air sinks

192

★★★ Keypoint.

SUMMARY OF COOKING METHODS

Way in which heat is applied	Method of cooking	Definition	Examples
Dry heat	Baking	Cooking carried out in an oven	Potatoes, fish, cakes
	Roasting	Baking with the addition of fat	Large joints of tender meat, potatoes
	Grilling	Using direct radiant heat	Small cuts of tender meat, e.g. chops and steak; fish
Moist heat	Boiling	Using boiling water	Eggs, large joints of tough meat, vegetables, fish
	Stewing and poaching	Using hot water below its boiling point	Meat in stews and hot pots. Fruit, fish, eggs
	Steaming	Using steam from boiling water	Fish, vegetables, suet puddings
	Pressure cooking	Using water boiling above its normal boiling point	Meat, vegetables such as beetroot which cook slowly in boiling water. In general used for foods which take a long time to cook by normal boiling or steaming
Fat	Frying	Using hot fat	Meat, often as rissoles or sausages. Potatoes, eggs, fish
Infra-red cooking	Equivalent to rapid grilling	Using infra-red radiation	Small tender cuts of meat

thus causing a flow of hot air through the oven. This movement of hot air is an example of convection. When food is cooked in hot water, the water circulates and heat is carried to the food by convection (though the food absorbs this heat by conduction).

3. Radiation. Hot bodies such as the sun send out heat by radiation. This radiant heat passes through space (like light) and heats

193

objects placed in its path. For example, in Fig. 47 radiant heat from the grill falls on the food in the grill-pan and as this heat is absorbed the food warms up. Radiant heat is also important in oven cooking.

★ ? How is heat transferred to food in the following examples: (1) toasting bread, (2) boiling potatoes and (3) baking potatoes? ★ ? In convection ovens the natural circulation of hot air is accelerated by means of a fan. The purpose of such an oven is to speed up cooking; why does a convection oven have this effect?

Microwave cooking

In ordinary cooking heat is applied to the outside food and it gradually penetrates to the inside. In *microwave cooking* heat is generated *within* the food when microwaves penetrate the food, are absorbed by water molecules in the food and converted into heat. Thus the whole food heats up very quickly. Microwaves can only penetrate food to a depth of 3–5 cm; thus small pieces of food are cooked very quickly indeed. Larger pieces of food are cooked more slowly, however, because where the microwaves cannot penetrate the food it is heated by conduction.

Advantages. 1. It is very quick. For example, a fish fillet is cooked in only 30 seconds, a chop in one minute, a chicken in two minutes and a baked potato in four minutes. 2. Pre-cooked food can be reheated rapidly when required. This is especially useful in fast food establishments such as snack bars, canteens and hospitals. 3. Frozen food can be defrosted rapidly and then cooked.

Disadvantages. 1. Cooking times must be carefully controlled. 2. Metal containers cannot be used as they reflect microwaves. Pottery, china, glass and paper containers are all suitable. 3. Some foods look and taste different. For example, food does not turn brown or become crisp. Meat may have a chewy texture and does not brown. Bacon is not crisp.

Slow cooking

The use of microwave ovens and pressure cookers is intended to speed up cooking but recently cookers designed to slow down the

194

cooking process have been introduced. Slow cookers (see photo) are electrically heated and made of a material with good insulating properties such as earthenware so that heat transfer to the food is slow and a steady temperature is maintained during cooking. Slow cookers work on low power—about that of a 100 watt light bulb—so that the cooking temperature remains below 100°C. The result is that food is cooked at a low even temperature over a long period—usually 4–6 hours. Slow cookers are much more economical to operate than conventional ovens. Recently domestic cookers having ovens capable of operating at low temperatures have become available so extending the range of slow cooking appliances.

Slow cookers are ideal for cooking cheaper, tougher cuts of meat. Such meat needs to be cooked slowly at a low temperature if it is to become tender (see page 217). Such cooking reduces weight loss by evaporation and prevents loss of juices because the slow cooker is sealed and no moisture escapes. For the reasons just mentioned slow cookers are ideal for cooking casseroles and stews. They may, however, be used to cook a wide range of dishes from roast meat to rice pudding. They have obvious benefits for working housewives who may put the cooker on at breakfast time and leave it unattended until supper time.

Effects of cooking on different nutrients

During cooking great changes take place in the nature of food, and some of these changes will be discussed in the next two chapters. Different foods behave in different ways on cooking but before we consider individual foods it will be helpful if we discuss the effect of heat on nutrients. These effects apply to all foods and if we understand them it will enable us to understand better the general principles of cooking. Then we shall be able to understand why a particular food or dish is cooked in one way rather than another.

1. Fats. When fats are heated they melt and if they contain water, this is driven off as water vapour. At 100°C fats containing water appear to boil; this is caused by the water being given off as steam. Fats are stable to heat and can be heated almost to their boiling point before they start to break down. It is because of this fact— and also because they have high boiling points—that fats are used

The Tower Slo-Cooker has a capacity of 3½ litres and may be used to cook a wide range of dishes from casseroles and roast meat to rice pudding and egg custard.

for cooking. When fats are heated too much, they break down producing an unpleasant-smelling smoke. Fat on the outside of meat and in bacon darkens in colour on strong heating and if the temperature is too high some breakdown and charring may occur.

2. *Carbohydrates*. Using dry heat, carbohydrates are broken down and darken in colour. For example, sucrose browns on caramelization and finally chars and becomes black, while starch is broken down into more easily digested *dextrins* and also darkens and eventually chars. Many foods that contain both sugars and protein turn golden brown and change flavour on heating. These changes occur in the toasting of bread and the baking of bread, cakes and biscuits, and contribute to the pleasant flavour and attractive colour of these products.

196

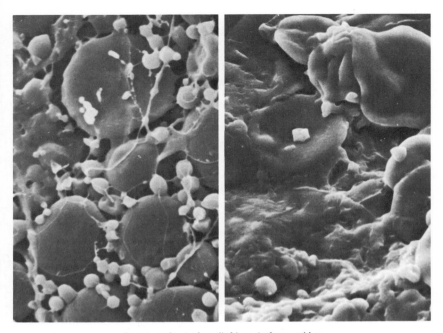

Starch grains before (left) and after cooking

When a mixture of starch and water is heated (see p. 167) the starch granules absorb water and swell and *gelatinize*, forming a thick white paste. This is why starchy material—cornflour or wheat flour for example—is used to thicken sauces. On cooling, the paste sets and forms a gel.

Uncooked starchy foods are difficult to digest because the digestive juices cannot penetrate into the starch grains. Cooking causes the starch granules to swell and gelatinize, making digestion easier. This change can be appreciated from the photos which show what raw starch granules look like under the microscope and how the granules swell and merge during cooking becoming soft and gelatinous in texture.

The polysaccharides starch, cellulose and pectin (see page 18) are important constituents of fruit and vegetables. On cooking, insoluble cellulose changes little, except to soften somewhat, whereas starch softens as it gelatinizes and pectin becomes more soluble and some dissolves, allowing cells to separate so making the fruit and vegetable easier to eat. Fruit with a high pectin content, such as apples, become soft and pulpy on cooking.

3. Proteins. Proteins undergo great changes when they are heated. Many proteins coagulate on being heated; you will remember that egg white coagulates when it is heated above 60°C. As proteins coagulate they become solid. For example, when milk is heated a skin forms, and this is because some of the proteins have coagulated. Cheese is another important protein food, and when it is heated it softens and on further heating some of the proteins coagulate and the cheese becomes stringy and tough.

Not all proteins coagulate on heating and this fact is important when considering how to cook protein foods. *Collagen* and *elastin*, for example, are two important insoluble proteins in meat and because they are not soluble they are not easily digested. Their presence in meat makes it tough, and as the cheaper cuts of meat usually contain more collagen and elastin than more expensive ones, they are usually tougher. Tough meat must be cooked in a way which will make it tender. If such meat is cooked at high temperatures for long periods it remains tough—or may even become tougher! Tough meat needs to be cooked slowly using low temperatures; both dry heat and moist heat methods may be used.

Tough meat is often cooked slowly using moist heat; by stewing for example. This converts the tough collagen into *gelatin*. Gelatin is a soluble protein—it is the substance which makes jellies set or 'gel'—and so is easily digested. It is now believed that slow cooking, using dry heat, is also effective in converting collagen into gelatin. Elastin softens on cooking, but not to the same extent as collagen.

4. Mineral elements. Heat does not affect mineral salts found in food, because they are stable substances which do not break down at the temperatures used in cooking. Moist heat methods of cooking, such as stewing and boiling, cause loss of salts which are soluble in water. Boiled fish, for example, is rather tasteless because of the considerable loss of mineral salts that occurs during cooking. However, the salts are present in the water in which the fish has been boiled, and this liquid or *stock* can be used for making a tasty sauce to eat with the fish.

HOW TO REDUCE THE LOSS OF VITAMIN C WHEN COOKING VEGETABLES

Precaution	Reason
1. Crush and chop vegetable as little as possible	Crushing and chopping release enzymes that help to destroy vitamin C in air
2. Put vegetables into boiling water	This destroys enzymes; boiling water does not contain oxygen
3. Use as little water as possible	The greater the amount of water used the greater is the loss of vitamin C into the cooking water
4. Cook for as short a time as possible	The longer the cooking time the greater the destruction of vitamin C
5. Cover the pan with a lid	Enables a small amount of water to be used. (see 3).
6. Do not add sodium bi-carbonate to improve colour	This substance is alkaline and increases destruction of vitamin C
7. Eat the vegetable immediately after cooking	Storing the vegetable hot can lead to complete destruction of vitamin C

5. Vitamins. Dry heat cooking methods destroy those vitamins which are unstable to heat. Vitamin C is destroyed at quite low temperatures, and so all methods of cooking cause some loss of this vitamin. To make the loss as small as possible, foods containing vitamin C should be cooked for as short a time as possible and should be eaten as soon as they are cooked. Two of the B vitamins, thiamine and riboflavin, are unstable at high temperatures. Riboflavin is the more stable of the two, and little is lost except at high cooking temperatures, such as those used in rapid grilling. Thiamine is largely destroyed at high temperatures, such as are used in grilling and roasting.

Cooking with moist heat causes loss of water-soluble vitamins, as well as those which are destroyed at low temperatures. Vitamin C is both soluble in water and unstable to heat, and therefore some loss during cooking cannot be avoided. Vitamin C is also destroyed by oxygen present in air and dissolved in cooking water. The rate of destruction is hastened by enzymes present in the plant or fruit. These enzymes are set free by crushing or chopping. When you cook vegetables you should take the precautions to reduce loss of vitamin C as shown in the table opposite.

The B vitamins are soluble in water in varying degrees, thiamine being the most soluble. A considerable proportion of the thiamine in foods may be lost during cooking, especially if they are boiled in alkaline solutions. For this reason you should not add an alkaline substance, such as sodium bicarbonate, to green vegetables to prevent loss of green colour during cooking. The amounts of the other B vitamins lost during cooking are small and not important.

Vitamin A and D are insoluble in water and stable except at high temperatures. There is therefore little, if any, loss of these vitamins during cooking.

11 Cooking II:
How to Cook; some important principles

This is not a cookery book, and we have no space to give recipes for cooking any particular dishes. There are many books which do give such recipes and you will find that they will help you to acquire skill in *how* to cook. However, it is important that you understand the basic ideas of cookery, the reasons *why* we cook particular foods in one way rather than another. You will be able to do this if you understand the nature of the foods discussed in earlier chapters and the effects of cooking on the different nutrients considered in the last chapter.

If you understand the reasons why we do things in cookery, you will not only find it easy to follow and understand recipes, but you will have enough knowledge to be able to take a basic recipe and adapt it in many varied and interesting ways. You will then have the thrill of being able to create your own recipes—you will be a *real* cook!

Egg cookery

Cooking eggs is very simple; egg cookery depends upon the nature of the proteins in the egg. As we have seen, when an egg is put into hot water the proteins coagulate and the egg gradually sets. Both dry and moist heat produce this effect, so that eggs coagulate during cooking whether they are being boiled or fried. Eggs are digestible in all forms, but they are most easily digested when the egg white is just solid and the yolk still liquid. If an egg is over-

"Why won't these cook?" **A real cook!**

Fig. 49. We need to know *why* we cook a food in a particular way

cooked, the white is hard and tough and the yolk breaks up into a powder.

✶✶Activity. *The right and wrong way to hard boil an egg.* Cook two eggs (a) one at about 90°C for 10 minutes which should then be cooled in cold water and (b) one fast boiled at 100°C for 20 minutes and allowed to cool slowly in air. When cold cut the eggs in half and examine. Prolonged heating at a high temperature toughens the protein and causes a purplish ring to form round the yolk. (Iron from the yolk and sulphur compounds from the white form iron sulphide.) What is the best way to hard boil an egg?

Eggs can be cooked in a wide variety of ways, all of which are simple and quick. Apart from boiling and frying they can be scrambled, poached and baked or made into omelets, soufflés and custards. Eggs are normally cooked at a low temperature for a short time so that the protein is coagulated but soft. The exception to this is in making omelets when the egg is whisked with a little water and salt and poured into a shallow pan containing a little very hot fat. The object is to form a thin foamy layer of coagulated egg quickly. If cooking is continued too long an unpleasant tough pancake results!

★ **?** How would you make scrambled egg so that it is soft and creamy? What would happen if you had to keep it hot for ten minutes?

★★★ **Keypoint.** The basis of cooking eggs is the effect of heat on

202

the proteins in the egg. Heat causes the protein to set or coagulate. Too much heat or too long cooking causes the egg protein to coagulate too much; this produces a tough effect.

Eggs are useful ingredients in cooking many types of dish, because of the setting effect that occurs when the egg proteins coagulate. Eggs used in cake mixtures, for example, help to 'fix' the shape of the cake during baking. Eggs in sauces and custards act as thickening agents.

Foods which are likely to break up during frying, such as fish cakes or rissoles, are often coated with egg and a dry starchy material—usually flour or browned breadcrumbs—before cooking. The egg-starchy mixture helps to bind the food on cooking for when the food is fried the egg coagulates and forms a hard coating that seals the surface and prevents the food from falling apart. It also prevents the food from absorbing too much fat and becoming greasy.

Egg whites in cookery

When egg white is beaten it becomes stiff because of the partial coagulation of the albumin. If this stiff foam is gently heated more coagulation occurs and it becomes rigid. This fact is very useful in cooking because it enables *foam* structures to be created. During the beating or whipping of egg white the protein is stretched out in the form of a film which encloses air in the form of tiny bubbles. The foam structure thus created is very light and when heated the foam sets as the protein coagulates further. This is the basis of making meringues and soufflés and of the use of eggs to give volume and lightness to sponge cakes and other baked goods.

★★ **Activity.** *Meringues.* (See photographs on page 204.)

(a) Take two egg whites at room temperature and whisk them until they are stiff. Add about 50 g caster sugar and whisk until the foam is stiff again. Add a further 50 g caster sugar and whisk until the foam is glossy and will form peaks that stand firm. Pipe the mixture onto an oiled tray, making each meringue the same size. Put in a warm place to set (e.g. an airing cupboard or a cool oven below 90°C).

(b) Repeat the above but add 1–2 g tartaric acid to the egg whites before whisking.

In making meringues egg whites are used to produce a stable foam that is coagulated by very gentle heating. 1. Egg whites are whisked briskly until they form a stiff foam that forms peaks. 2. The caster sugar is added in stages and the mixture is whisked until stiff again. 3. The final mixture should be a smooth foam with a glossy appearance

Can you detect any difference in the appearance, texture or number of meringues made in (a) and (b)?

Discussion. The making of meringues illustrates some of the properties of proteins. Whisking stretches the protein and forms

204

a foam of tiny air bubbles. Warming coagulates the protein film and fixes or sets the meringue. Addition of sugar strengthens the foam (as well as improving flavour). Addition of an acid increases the rate at which protein coagulates and aids foam development and stability. It should therefore increase the total volume and hence the number of meringues made. It also improves whiteness. This activity illustrates how conditions of cooking affect protein foods. The addition of a little acid or salt promotes coagulation as well as heating and beating and you will see how this is important in cooking other protein foods later on in the chapter.

★★ **Activity.** Repeat the activity (a) above but allow a little egg yolk to be mixed with the egg white. You should find that you cannot produce a stable foam; even a trace of fat (present in the yolk) is enough to cause a foam to collapse.

★ ? In some recipes for making meringues a pinch of salt is added. What benefit could this have? In poaching eggs vinegar may be added to the cooking water. Why is this?

Whole eggs in cookery

★★★ **Keypoint.** Egg white is nothing more than a little protein in water (see page 24) but the yolk is a much richer source of nutrients and contains fat as well as protein. The fat is in the form of an emulsion. It follows that whole eggs have a higher food value than egg white and that because of the emulsified fat they contain they behave rather differently in cooking from egg white.

★ ? Do eggs contain anything else besides proteins, fat and water?

Whole eggs can be used in cooking as thickening agents. Coagulation starts at about 70°C, though if other ingredients, such as sugar and milk are added as in making a custard, coagulation doesn't start until about 80°C. In using whole eggs to make a thick custard the object is to coagulate the mixture until it just sets into a *gel* e.g. above about 80°C, it *curdles* (see page 80) and the custard is ruined. You will see that temperature needs to be carefully controlled in making custards.

★★ **Activity.** *Baked Custard.* A baked custard is a mixture of eggs, milk and sugar. It should just coagulate to give a firm but smooth gel. (a) Heat $\frac{1}{2}$ pint of milk to about 65°C. Beat 1 whole egg with about 15 g sugar, add the hot milk and stir. Pour into a dish standing in a pan of water and bake in a very cool oven of about 175°C for 30 to 40 minutes. (b) Repeat but boil the milk and bake for one hour at an oven temperature of 200°C. Record the appearance, texture and taste in (a) and (b).

When milk is heated too much it curdles and when a custard is heated at too high a temperature the proteins contract and liquids separate out from the gel thus spoiling the texture.

★ ? What would happen to a baked custard if the amount of milk used was increased compared to the amount of eggs? Why?
★ ? In making a baked custard why is the cooking dish placed in a pan of water? Could you make the custard successfully without using the pan of water?

The thickening effect of whole eggs is also used in making soufflés (see photo below) which are similar to baked custards

A **Cheese Soufflé.** A soufflé is similar to a baked custard but is light and fluffy in texture because the egg whites are whisked to form a foam and egg yolks are beaten and added to a flour sauce

except that they are whisked to give them a light foamy structure, and starch is used to give an additional thickening effect. A variety of puddings can be made based on egg custards, in which flour, cornflour or gelatin are used as additional thickening agents.

BAKING

Baked goods are made from wheat flour (see page 57) mixed with water or milk to which other ingredients, such as eggs, fat and sugar may have been added. The other essential ingredient is a raising or aerating agent that causes the mixture to expand (rise) during baking to give the finished product its typical light texture. The three main types of baked goods are shown in the table below.

TYPES OF BAKED GOODS

Type	Description	Examples
Batter	A liquid mixture that is beaten and can be poured	Pancakes Cakes
Paste	Firmer than a batter, contains fat; mixed to a consistency that can be rolled	Puff pastry Short pastry Biscuits
Dough	Thicker than a paste so requires careful mixing (see photo 2 on page 62); contains less fat than a paste	Bread Rolls Buns

The principles of making baked goods can be illustrated by describing how bread can be made from flour, water, yeast and salt. You can see how bread is made on a large scale by turning back to page 62, and a method for making home-made bread is given in the table on page 209).

Making bread

When flour and water are mixed together, dough is formed and proteins in the flour form an elastic substance called *gluten*, which

A selection of bread rolls. 1. Croissants. 2. Brioche. 3. Baps. 4. A selection including three types covered with poppy seeds and (*top right*) a Vienna roll

binds together the flour in the dough. In biblical times this dough was simply baked to give a hard and unattractive product called *unleavened bread*. In order to make bread as we know it to-day, the dough must be made lighter by puffing it up with gas. This process is called *aeration*.

The gas used for aeration is carbon dioxide, and it is produced by *fermentation*. Fermentation processes are brought about by enzymes and in this case the enzymes are contained within very small living cells of yeast. Yeast cells are too small to be seen with the naked eye, but they are clearly visible through a microscope. They live and multiply by using the protein of the dough as food. They also use the sugars present in the dough to obtain energy. In using the sugar they break it down into carbon dioxide and *alcohol*, the substance which is present in all alcoholic drinks, such as beer and wines. The carbon dioxide produced in this way becomes trapped in the dough as small pockets of gas.

The stages of making home made bread are shown in the table

★★ Activity. Making a bread by a quick method.

Stages	Description
Ingredients	250 g bread flour (plain and strong), 7 g fresh yeast, 150 cm^3 water, 1 teaspoon salt, 10 g ascorbic acid
Yeast mixture	Crumble yeast into warm water (30–35°C), add sugar and ascorbic acid; mix well
Mixing	Mix flour and salt in a warm bowl and add warm yeast mixture. Mix into a smooth dough
Kneading	Turn out dough onto a floured board, knead for 10 minutes
Proving	Return dough to bowl, cover, leave in warm place for 5 minutes
Moulding	Mould into shape required for rolls or loaf and place under greased polythene or in greased tin
Reproving	Allow to prove in warm place for about 30 minutes until well risen
Baking	Bake in hot oven (225°C) for about 40 minutes (loaf) or 20 minutes (rolls)

★★★ Keypoints.

1. *Yeast.* There are three types of yeast: *fresh* or *compressed yeast* which is best for making bread. It can be stored in a cold place for 2–3 days or kept in a freezer until required; *brewer's yeast* which has a strong taste and does not keep well; *dried yeast* which can be stored indefinitely if kept dry and sealed but which takes longer to ferment.
2. *Flour improvers.* Ascorbic acid is an example of a *flour improver*. It makes the gluten stronger and more elastic.
3. *Temperature.* The yeast mixture, dry ingredients, mixing bowl and dough should be kept warm (25–35°C) at all times. Too low a temperature slows down yeast activity and too high a temperature kills yeast cells.
4. *Milk.* Water may be replaced by milk or a milk–water mixture. It improves flavour and food value and makes the crust browner.
5. *Fat.* 10 g fat (lard or margarine) may be added by rubbing it into the flour. It increases the tenderness of crust and crumb as well as improving flavour.
6. *Salt.* This strengthens and toughens the gluten and improves flavour.

209

on p. 209. Once the dough has risen to the required size due to the action of the yeast, it is put into the oven to be baked. In the oven the dough first rises rapidly because the pockets of trapped gas expand as the gas gets hot. Fermentation continues until the temperature of the aerated dough reaches about 60°C. At this temperature the yeast cells are killed.

The gradual expansion of the dough is made possible because of the elastic nature of the gluten. As gluten is made from proteins, it coagulates when it gets hot. Thus during baking the elasticity of the loaf is lost and its shape becomes fixed. The nature of the starch also changes as it gets hot. It absorbs water to such an extent that the starch grains swell. Owing to the high temperature on the outside of the loaf, the starch is converted into a hard crust which, if baked sufficiently, is crisp and golden-brown in colour.

Bread is cooked for 30–50 minutes, depending upon its size, and the result is the familiar loaf of bread—so familiar in fact that we are apt to forget that it has needed much skill and effort to produce it from those fields of golden wheat.

★★ **Activity.** *Gluten.* Wheat flour contains proteins that form gluten. When gluten is mixed with water it forms an elastic dough, that will stretch without breaking. The proteins of gluten coagulate on baking to give a firm structure to the loaf. Wrap a little wheat flour in muslin and put in a basin of water. Work the flour with your hands until the water is milky in appearance, then wash the muslin under a cold tap working it with your fingers. Continue until the water is clear. You have now washed out the starch leaving the gluten behind. Carry out the following tests: (a) Pull a little gluten about in your fingers. What is it like? (b) Heat a little in a flame. Note the smell. What does it indicate? (c) Bake a little gluten in a hot oven. Observe the result. What has happened?

★★★ **Keypoint.** Strong flours contain more gluten than weak ones (see table on page 58). A strong flour with high gluten content is used for baked goods such as bread which must rise considerably on baking, whereas a soft flour with low gluten content is used for cakes and biscuits which rise less and require less of ingredients that contribute to structure.

Rich cakes

There are many varieties of rich cakes so we shall take one example to illustrate the main principles involved in cooking them. The traditional 'pound cake' is made from one pound of each of the four ingredients—fat, sugar, flour and eggs.

A cake recipe is chosen so that the ingredients which give volume to the final product are balanced by those that give strength to its structure. If the ingredients giving volume are present in too small a proportion, the cake does not rise properly during baking and the product is too solid. If they are present in too large a proportion, the cake mixture rises rapidly during baking but later collapses, so that the cake sinks in the middle (Fig. 50).

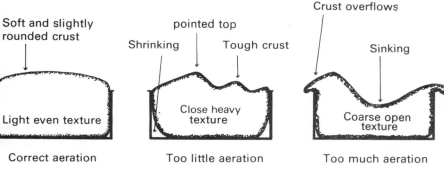

Fig. 50. Aeration of a cake mixture

In the pound cake, the egg white and fat provide volume by trapping air in the mixture while the flour (which forms gluten) and eggs produce a strong structure. Sugar makes the product sweet, and also improves texture.

In order to make this rich type of cake the fat—butter for preference—is softened (but *not* melted) and then mixed with the sugar. The mixture is beaten up until it is smooth, white and fluffy. This is called *creaming*, and during beating air becomes trapped in the mixture. The eggs, well beaten, may then be added, and the mixture is again beaten until it is light and foamy. The flour is gently folded in, and the mixture gently stirred until blending is complete and the mixture smooth.

The mixture is put into the oven, pre-heated to the required temperature, and cooked in a tin which has been greased and lined

211

with greaseproof paper. During baking, the bubbles of air and water vapour trapped in the mixture expand and the cake rises. These bubbles are enclosed in an oily film containing egg white proteins, and as these proteins coagulate the film becomes rigid and the shape of the cake is 'fixed'. When baking is complete the cake structure is light, open and strong.

★★★ **Keypoint.** In a cake recipe ingredients that give *volume* have to be balanced with those that give *strength*.

★ ? In a pound cake what ingredients contribute to volume and what to structure? Why is no raising agent needed?

Raising agents

Most cake mixtures contain a larger proportion of flour than a pound cake, and in such cases increased aeration is needed. This is supplied by a *raising agent*.

Baking soda or *sodium bicarbonate* is the simplest raising agent. When it is heated it breaks down producing carbon dioxide, which aerates the product. Unfortunately it also produces *sodium carbonate*, better known as washing soda. This substance is left behind in the mixture being baked, and, if present in large amounts, gives it an unpleasant taste. So baking soda is best used in making baked products like ginger bread and chocolate cake, which have a strong flavour of their own.

For most purposes a *baking powder* is a more suitable raising agent than baking soda. It consists of a mixture of substances which produce carbon dioxide when mixed with water and heated. Baking powders are made from baking soda, an acid substance— often either *tartaric acid* or *cream of tartar*—and some form of starch as a filler.

As long as a baking powder is kept dry it will keep well, and if it does get slightly damp, the moisture is absorbed by the filler. When it is mixed with water and heated, the baking soda reacts with the acid substance and carbon dioxide is produced.

Stages in making a rich fruit cake. (1) Sieve the flour (and spice). (2) Clean the fruit and chop the peel and cherries. Blanch and chop the almonds. (3) Beat the soft butter or margarine till creamy, add the sugar and beat till light and fluffy. (4) Add the eggs one at a time and beat well. Mix in the sieved flour. (5) Stir in other dry ingredients gently. (6) Put the mixture into a well-lined tin, and cook in a slow oven (190°C reducing to about 150°C)

Fig. 51. Cake textures, showing the small regular bubbles in a well-baked cake and the large uneven bubbles if too much baking powder is used

It is important that the correct amount of baking powder is added to a mixture; too much is just as bad as too little (Fig. 51). As a matter of convenience a *self-raising flour* is sometimes used. As its name suggests this is flour to which a certain amount of baking powder has been added. The proportion of baking powder is such that self-raising flour is suitable for plain cakes and scones—but *not* for rich cakes. It has the disadvantage that the ratio of baking powder to flour is fixed. When you gain confidence in making cakes you will prefer to use plain flour and calculate for yourself the best amount of baking powder to use.

Plain cakes

A rich cake is one in which the weight of fat is *more* than half the weight of flour. In a very rich cake, such as the pound cake considered earlier, the weight of fat equals the weight of flour. In very rich cakes—see table overleaf—the weight of flour also equals the weight of egg. As an egg can aerate its own weight of flour, such cakes need no baking powder. As a cake mixture becomes plainer the proportion of flour to that of fat (and eggs) increases, and in general a plain cake is one in which the weight of fat is *less* than half the weight of flour. In plain cakes eggs cannot provide enough aeration, and baking powder must be used. In the plainest mixtures, such as scones, baking powder provides all the aeration, and so a greater amount is needed.

In making a plain cake the flour is sifted into a dry basin and baking powder and salt added. The fat is rubbed into the flour very thoroughly, until the mixture looks like fine breadcrumbs. The sugar and other dry ingredients, such as fruit and flavouring, are added and the whole is mixed to the right consistency with the beaten eggs and milk. The mixture should be semi-fluid so that it will not pour, but may be dropped from a spoon into a greased tin. It is baked in a moderately hot oven.

INGREDIENTS OF CAKES: COMPARATIVE WEIGHTS

Plain flour (g)	Fats (g)	Sugar (g)	No. of Eggs	Fruit (g)	Liquid milk (pt)	Basic recipe	Baking powder (level tea-spoons)
200	37	As required	—	Optional	$\frac{1}{4}$ approx.	Scone	4
200	75	75	1	75 to 100	$\frac{1}{4}$ approx.	Plain cake	3
200	150	150	3	150 to 200	A little	Rich cake	1
200	200	200	4	200 to 250	A little	Very rich cake	—

Choice and purpose of cake ingredients

1. Flour. Flour is the basis of all cakes and so it is obviously just as important to choose the right *sort* of flour as to use the right *amount*. Flour is called *strong* if it contains a large amount of gluten (more than 10%), and *weak* or *soft* if it contains a small amount. During baking gluten coagulates so giving strength to the mixture. A weak flour is best for cakes as it gives a fine even texture. Plain or household flour, which is the sort commonly used, is a blend of strong and weak flours, and though satisfactory for making cakes, does not give such a fine texture as a weak one.

2. Sugar. Sugar gives cakes a sweet flavour and improves texture. Caster sugar is the best variety for most light cakes, because its small crystals dissolve easily during mixing; it also creams well to give a smooth texture. Sugar also adds colour to the crust and improves keeping quality.

3. Fat. Fat for use in cakes should have the following qualities: it should cream well so that the cake mixture is smooth and light; fat therefore contributes to volume by helping to aerate the mix

215

during creaming. It should make the cake 'short' or tender by coating the starch in the flour with an oily film so that the baked cake 'melts' in the mouth; it should be neither too hard nor too soft—and it should have a good flavour. Of the fats used in cake making, such as margarine, butter and lard, butter is the best.

4. Eggs. Egg white assists in trapping air and in moistening the cake mixture; it also adds strength to the structure when it coagulates on baking. Egg yolk adds richness and colour. Eggs used in cakes should be fresh and of good quality.

5. Fruit. Dried fruit adds sweetness and flavour to cakes. Fruit should be washed and dried before being added to the mixture (and stones should be removed if present). Also care should be taken to see that the mixture is stiff enough to support the fruit or the fruit will sink to the bottom of the cake.

★★ **Activity.** *Making sponge cake.* In a rich pound cake air is incorporated by creaming together eggs, fat and sugar. As we have seen above the fat contributes to aeration as well as adding richness and tenderness. It is possible to make a cake, however, without the use of any fat, using eggs as the aerating agent. Sponge cakes and Angel cake are the main examples.

(a) Put four eggs and 150 g sugar into a basin standing in hot water. Whisk until the mixture is very *firm*, light and fluffy. Remove from the hot water and gently fold in 100 g sieved flour a little at a time. Pour the mixture into a prepared tin and bake in a moderate oven (175°C) for about one hour. (b) Repeat (a) but reduce the whisking time and stop beating the mixture when a foam is just formed.

★ ? 1. Which sponge cake was the most successful? Why?
  2. Why was no raising agent used in making sponge cake?
  3. What factors produced aeration in sponge cake?
  4. What factors gave strength to the structure?
  5. Remove the hot sponge cake from the oven after one hour. Break off a piece. Is the hot cake delicate or strong? Should it be cooled before being taken out of the pan?
  6. When the sponge cakes are cool cut them in half. Describe their texture and taste them. Which has the better taste and texture?

7. Why is the flour folded into the mixture as gently as possible? What would be the effect of beating or stirring?

In making sponge cakes the lightness of the cake depends on successful aeration produced by the eggs. The utmost care is therefore needed to produce a stable foam, and for this reason whisking must be continued until the foam is very stiff. When the cake is baked the air trapped in the stable foam plus steam from the liquid contained in the eggs produce the necessary aeration. The structure of such cakes is delicate because it is due mainly to coagulation of the egg proteins during baking.

★ ? What would be the effect of reducing the proportion of eggs in a sponge cake mixture?

Meat

Meat is cooked to make it tender, to give it a good flavour and to make it safe by killing bacteria. As we saw on page 197 rapid cooking can only be used for tender meat. Tender cuts of meat may be roasted, grilled or fried. If a low temperature is used, soluble proteins gradually coagulate and the red colour of raw meat slowly changes to the dark brown colour of cooked meat. The proteins of the connective tissues start to shrink causing some of the 'juice' in the meat to be squeezed out. If the meat is being roasted in an open container, its surface becomes dry as moisture evaporates. This dryness can be avoided by *basting*, i.e. covering the meat with a little oil from time to time.

If a high temperature is used the cooking time is reduced. High temperature cooking rapidly *sears* the surface of the meat giving it a dark brown appearance and causing much shrinkage of connective tissue, and loss of juice. Soluble proteins tend to be more completely coagulated, and therefore harder and less digestible. Such cooking gives a rather dry and hard but well-flavoured surface to the meat.

Rapid cooking methods do not make meat more tender because, as we have seen, the insoluble proteins collagen and elastin, which make meat tough, are not softened. Tough meat must therefore be cooked very slowly; for example, by stewing or *slow* roasting. Such cooking converts collagen into soluble gelatin.

Cooking with moist heat is slow, soluble proteins being coagulated only slowly and collagen being slowly converted into gelatin. Soluble nutrients, mainly mineral salts and thiamine, and *meat extractives*—which are the flavouring agents that give meat its special flavour—pass into the cooking water. Boiled or stewed meat is therefore less tasty than roasted meat. This is not usually important, however, because the liquor in which the meat is cooked is usually eaten with the meat. In making a stew or hot pot, the meat is cut into small pieces and the cooking liquor is used for cooking vegetables, herbs and spices which are eaten with the meat.

Because normal moist heat cooking of meat is slow, a pressure cooker may conveniently be used to make it quicker. For example, an Irish stew which takes two hours to cook by simmering, only takes about a quarter of an hour in a pressure cooker.

Ways of making meat tender

✳✳✳ Keypoint. Meat which is tough is cooked very slowly as this breaks down the insoluble protein collagen contained in the tough connective tissue and converts it to gelatin. The other insoluble protein in connective tissue—elastin—is only softened by moist heat cooking and additional methods are needed to make the meat really tender.

1. As an animal becomes older the connective tissue increases and the muscle fibres become thicker and tougher. Exercise has the same effect. In selecting meat therefore it is important to consider its quality. Meat with a fine texture and little thick connective tissue will be the most tender.
2. Meat from freshly killed animals should not be cooked until it has been stored or hung for some time. During this time tenderness and flavour increase. Storing is particularly important for beef and for poultry and game.
3. Tenderness can be improved by mechanical pounding, by scoring with a knife and by cutting or chopping into pieces. All these break up the elastin into small pieces and thus make the meat easier to chew. In stewing, for example, the meat is normally cut into small pieces before being cooked.
4. Meat can be made more tender by the use of *tenderizers*. These substances contain enzymes that break down protein. The juice from the papaya fruit, for example, contains the enzyme

papain (pronounced pap-ay-in) which acts on protein in a similar way to the digestive protein-splitting enzymes in the body. Such a tenderizer may be injected into an animal just before it is killed, or it may be added to the surface of the meat just before it is cooked. Care must be taken not to add too much tenderizer or not only is the connective tissue broken down but also too much muscle fibre giving the meat a soft mushy texture.

5. The tenderness of meat can be improved by the addition of an acid substance, such as lemon juice, vinegar or tomato juice. The acid increases the rate at which collagen is converted into gelatin, but it does not affect the elastin. Addition of an acid alone cannot, therefore, make meat tender. The method used is usually to soak (marinate) the meat in an acid solution (marinade) for several days before cooking. For example, beef which is to be braised may be soaked in a vinegar marinade to which wine and spices are added to improve flavour. The marinade can be used as part of the liquid in which the meat is cooked.

★★ **Activity.** Suggest ways in which you might cook (a) a thin beef steak, (b) pork chops, (c) shoulder of lamb, (d) neck of mutton.

★ ? Why is meat cooked? What are the advantages of using moist heat?

★ ? In making a stew vegetables are cooked with the meat. Why are the vegetables only added towards the end of the cooking period? Why is meat to be stewed cut up into small pieces?

★★ **Activity.** Cut up a piece of tough meat into three small pieces. Observe the colour of the freshly cut meat and the texture. Put one piece into cold water, one piece into cold water after rubbing a tenderizer into the surface, and one piece into boiling water. Heat them all and note any changes. After half an hour cut each piece of meat, note which is the most tender, and chew each. Did the use of tenderizer have any effect? Was the cooking time long enough?

Fish

The changes which occur when fish is cooked are similar to those which take place when meat is cooked. As fish contains less con-

219

nective tissue than meat and no elastin it is much less tough, and cooking is not needed to make it tender, but only to make it more palatable.

Fish may be cooked using dry or moist heat. If dry heat is used soluble proteins are coagulated and some shrinkage occurs. Fish shrinks less than meat because of the smaller amount of connective tissue that it contains. As fish shrinks water evaporates from its surface leaving behind a deposit of flavouring matter and mineral salts. This makes the surface of the cooked fish very tasty.

If fish is cooked using moist heat, for instance by steaming or poaching, loss of soluble matter is greater than in dry heat methods. As fish contains less mineral salts and extractives than meat, such fish tends to be rather tasteless. It is usually eaten with a tasty sauce, which may be made from the liquor in which the fish was cooked.

★ ? Why does fish require less cooking than meat?

★★★ **Keypoint.** Whereas it is the degree of toughness that decides how meat is best cooked, it is the fat content of fish that decides how it should be cooked.

From Fig. 36 on page 96 you can see which fish contain much fat. All fish can be cooked by steaming or baking, but fat fish such as herring are best not deep fried because this makes the result too fatty. Such fish can be shallow fried as this causes less fat to be absorbed or they can be baked or grilled. Lean fish such as cod can be deep fried as this adds richness, or they can be poached or baked.

★ ? How would you cook (a) plaice, (b) salmon, (c) cod cutlets? Would you serve a sauce with any of these? Why?

Vegetables

All vegetable material is made up of cells that are enclosed by walls made up of cellulose together with some insoluble pectin, that acts as a sort of cement holding the cells together. Within the cell the main substance is water together with some protein and a variety of other nutrients, notably starch in potatoes and the pulses (beans, peas, lentils) and mineral elements and vitamins in

220

Potatoes are cooked to gelatinize the starch grains, make pectin more soluble and soften cellulose. This occurs in both dry and moist cooking methods, so that they may be cooked and served in a large number of ways.

leafy vegetables (cabbage, spinach) and fruits. As plant cells grow older lignin, which is tough and woody in texture, develops. Lignin is responsible for the stringiness of old runner beans, the woody texture of old carrots and the gritty parts of ripe plums.

When vegetables are cooked the cells are killed and the proteins in the cells coagulate. This allows water to escape from the cells, causing the vegetables to lose their crisp texture. Vegetables soften on cooking, partly because the cellulose softens, but mainly because the starch gelatinizes (p. 197) becoming soft and jelly-like and the pectin becomes more soluble, so making it easier for the cells to fall apart on eating.

✶ ? What are the main reasons why vegetables are cooked?

✶ ? Why do old vegetables need more cooking than young ones?

Cooking causes important changes in the colour, texture and flavour of vegetables (see next Chapter).

Green vegetables should be cooked until their texture has been softened enough to make them *just* tender. Cooking should be carried out in such a way that as much vitamin C as possible is preserved (see page 199). As little water as possible should be used to reduce the amount of nutrients and flavourings lost to the cooking water. The only exception to this is with vegetables that have a strong flavour which should be cooked in plenty of water. Strong-flavoured green vegetables include Brussels sprouts and broccoli. These vegetables should be cooked for as short a time as possible to give a pleasant mild flavour and good texture. Other strongly flavoured vegetables such as onions should also be cooked in plenty of water, but should be cooked for a longer time otherwise the flavour is too sharp.

Uncooked *starchy vegetables*, such as potatoes, are difficult to digest because the digestive juices cannot penetrate the starch grains (see Fig. 52). Groups of starch grains in raw potatoes are enclosed within the walls of the plant cell which is made of cellulose together with some pectin in and between the cell walls, so as the potatoes are cooked in water, starch grains swell and gelatinize, cellulose is somewhat softened and pectin becomes more soluble. Further heating completes gelatinization, giving the potatoes a soft texture; also loss of pectin causes the cells to separate easily, so making the potatoes easier to eat. As potatoes are about four-fifths water, starch grains are gelatinized by both dry and moist heating methods. Potatoes may therefore be cooked by any method,

★★★ **Keypoint.**

SUMMARY OF EFFECT OF COOKING ON NUTRIENTS

Nutrient	Effect of moist heat	Effect of dry heat
Fats	Melt to oil	Melt to oil. At very high temperatures smoke, then burn
Carbohydrates		
Starch	Starch grains absorb moisture, swell and gelatinize	Converted to dextrins, char
Cellulose	Softens somewhat	—
Pectin	Becomes soluble	—
Sugar	Forms syrup, turns to caramel, chars	Converted to caramel, chars
Proteins	Many proteins slowly coagulate, e.g. egg white. Insoluble proteins may be converted to soluble ones, e.g. collagen converted to gelatin, or unchanged, e.g. elastin	Many coagulate, e.g. albumin of egg white. Insoluble proteins may be hardened, e.g. collagen, or unchanged, e.g. elastin
Mineral salts	Soluble salts are partly lost to the cooking water	Most are stable to heat, a few break down, e.g. baking soda
Vitamins		
Vitamin A	Insoluble in water, not affected	Not affected
Thiamine	Soluble in water, some lost	Destroyed at high temperatures
Riboflavin	Slightly soluble in water, very little lost	Destroyed at very high temperatures
Vitamin C	Soluble in water, destroyed	Destroyed at low temperatures
Vitamin D	Insoluble in water, not affected	Not affected

with the result that they can be served in a large variety of ways.

If potatoes are boiled, mineral salts and vitamin C are lost to the cooking water. Additional amounts of vitamin C are destroyed by heat, so that peeled potatoes lose about half their vitamin C during boiling. To keep these losses as small as possible potatoes should be put into a minimum of boiling water so that enzymes are rapidly destroyed and loss of vitamin C into the cooking water is minimized. Cooking time may be reduced to 8–10 minutes by using a pressure cooker, and the loss of vitamin C is less. Pressure cookers are particularly useful for cooking vegetables, such as beetroot and artichokes, which take a long time to cook by boiling.

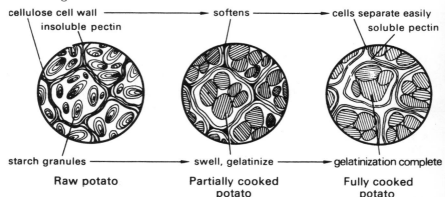

cellulose cell wall ⟶ softens ⟶ cells separate easily

insoluble pectin

soluble pectin

starch granules ⟶ swell, gelatinize ⟶ gelatinization complete

Raw potato   Partially cooked potato   Fully cooked potato

Fig. 52. Section of a potato before and during cooking as seen through a microscope

Frozen vegetables are now readily available and most of them are put into the cooking water while still frozen. Otherwise they are cooked in the same way as fresh vegetables, using the minimum amount of water. The time taken for cooking is about half that needed for the fresh variety, because before being frozen they are treated with boiling water or blanched (see page 162). Tests with peas and sprouts show that, when cooked until they are just tender, both fresh and frozen varieties retain about the same amount of Vitamin C, namely 55-60%.

★ ? What vegetables can you think of that are best eaten raw?
★ ? Why is boiling one of the most popular ways of cooking vegetables?
★ ? Why should vegetables be served and eaten immediately after cooking?

224

12 Cooking III:
Colour, Flavour and Texture

THE APPRECIATION OF FOOD

We eat food to live, but we also eat food for *enjoyment*. For most people food is one of the major pleasures of life and rightly so. We have already said in Chapter 7 that when you plan meals you must take care that they are attractive as well as of good food value.

★ ? What are the 'Top Ten' points for planning attractive meals? (Turn back to page 135 if you cannot remember.)

In food preparation and meal planning you must always remember that 'food is for eating'—it is not enough just to provide the right amount of nutrients, though of course this is important! You must also make sure that a meal is so attractive that it will be appreciated and enjoyed by those who eat it. So now let us think *how* we appreciate food.

★★★ **Keypoint.** We appreciate food through our senses:

Sight – Smell – Taste – Texture – Temperature

The table opposite will help you understand what this means.

★★ **Activity.** Taste a selection of foods and try to describe your appreciation of them in terms of your senses. The following pairs would be good ones to try: a slice of apple or cucumber and a slice of banana; a piece of bread and a biscuit; a sugar lump and a few crystals of salt; vinegar and salad cream; meat and fish; a hot lightly boiled egg and a cold hard boiled egg.

★★ Activity. Taste cornflakes, potato crisps and hard toast. Describe them in terms of your senses. What extra sense have you used that is not in the table? (Don't forget to use your ears!)

HOW WE APPRECIATE FOOD THROUGH OUR SENSES

Sense	Description	Examples
Sight	The appearance of food as sensed through the eyes. Colour and shape are important	Rice pudding looks uninteresting; strawberries and cream look exciting
Smell	The aroma of food as sensed through the nose	Cold coffee and cold meat have very little aroma; roasting coffee and roasting meat smell good
Taste	The taste of food as sensed by the mouth, e.g. its sweetness or sourness	Sugar tastes sweet; vinegar tastes sour
Texture	The feel of food as sensed by the mouth, e.g. its hardness or softness	Biscuits are crisp; nuts are hard; an instant whip is soft and smooth
Temperature	The hotness or coldness of food as sensed by the mouth	Cold and hot tea and cold and hot porridge are very different

When you cook food you must think what effect this will have on it; will it make it more or less attractive for example? In this chapter we are going to think about the colour, flavour and texture of food and of how cooking and food preparation in general affects these three.

★ **?** Do you think the following are more attractive if served cooked or uncooked; give your reasons.

Tomatoes, strawberries, lettuce, potatoes, onions, sausages, eggs.

226

COLOUR

We are very sensitive to the colour of the things around us; if you play tennis dressed in black clothes or if you get very suntanned or go very white when you are feeling ill people are very quick to notice (and make remarks!). We are also very sensitive to the colour of the food we eat. For example, pink bread, green cake and purple tomato sauce would not be very popular however nice they tasted. On the other hand, we enjoy freshly roasted meat that is a rich dark brown on the outside, and when we see a loaf of bread that has just come out of the oven we admire its crispy brown crust.

★★ **Activity.** The colour of food is an important factor in appreciating it, and it also affects our sense of flavour. Make up a series of gelatin jellies in the usual way using ordinary gelatin. Put a different edible colour in each and also a little flavour. For example, make up the following: a bright red jelly with a banana flavour; a green jelly with a raspberry flavour and an orange-coloured jelly with a lemon flavour. Get several people to taste them in turn and record what they think the flavour of each is. You will probably find they get them wrong because we associate a particular flavour with a particular colour. Raspberries are red

The attractiveness of baked goods such as these small cakes depends partly on their colour. Here the degree of browning is being measured against a set of standard colours

and so if a jelly is red we expect it to taste of raspberries or some other red fruit. Our senses are easily deceived, or so it seems!

The colour of fruit and vegetables

The bright colours of fresh fruit are one of their most attractive features; think, for example, of the colour of fresh strawberries or a rosy-red apple just picked off the tree. The table below describes the main colours found in fruit and vegetables.

THE COLOURS OF FRUIT AND VEGETABLES

Name	Colour	Examples
Chlorophyll	Green	Lettuce, cabbage (and green leafy vegetables in general)
Carotenoids	Yellow to red	Carrots, peaches, apricots, tomatoes, bananas
Flavonoids (a) Anthocyanins (b) Flavones	Red to voilet Yellow to white	Plums, strawberries (berry fruits in general) Apples, onions, cauli-flower

WAYS TO PREVENT 'BROWNING' OF FRUIT AND VEGETABLES

Principle	Treatment
Destroy enzymes	Put into very hot water (blanch)
Keep air out	Store in cold water or salt water
Use an acid	Keep in water made acid with lemon juice
Use of Vitamin C or sodium metabisulphite	Keep in water in which vitamin C or sodium metabisulphite has been dissolved

Once fruit and vegetables have been picked their colour starts to deteriorate; this is particularly true if they are bruised or cut, because this causes the release of *enzymes* that in the presence of air cause colour changes to occur. For example, apples, pears and potatoes all go brown if they are bruised or cut, and this makes them look very unattractive. Ways of preventing them from going brown are shown in the table on page 228.

★★ **Activity.** Peel and cut an apple or potato into slices. Immediately treat some slices in the four ways suggested in the table above. Leave the other slices in air and when they have turned brown observe the appearance of the treated slices. Leave the treated slices for a day or two and note their appearance. Which method preserves the original colour best?

★ ? When preparing boiled potatoes why should the potatoes normally be cooked immediately after being peeled? If they are not to be cooked immediately, how should they be stored?

When green vegetables are cooked the colour changes, and if they are cooked for a long time the original fresh green colour darkens to a dull olive green (or even brownish-green). This undesirable colour change is brought about by the action of heat and of acids present in the vegetable. If during cooking the lid of the pan is removed, some acids escape with the steam and so the colour change is less. If sodium bicarbonate (baking soda) is added to the cooking water it partly neutralizes the acids and so produces vegetables of a bright green colour. Unfortunately, sodium bicarbonate destroys vitamin C in vegetables, so that its use cannot be recommended.

★★ **Activity.** Cook three portions of cabbage, the first portion in an open pan, the second in a closed pan and the third in an open pan to which some sodium bicarbonate has been added. Use the same amount of water in each pan and cook each portion at the same rate. Note the colour of the cabbage in each pan at five-minute intervals over a period of thirty minutes. Which method retains the colour of the fresh vegetable best?

★★ **Activity.** Cook two portions of red cabbage, one in water to which sodium bicarbonate has been added and the other in water to which vinegar has been added. Note the colour of each portion of cabbage as it cooks. *Note.* The colour of red cabbage is due to the *anthocyanins* present (see table above). These substances have different colours in acids and alkalis.

Colours added to food

So far we have discussed colours which are found naturally in food, but sometimes colours are added to food to make its appearance more attractive. Some of these colours are *natural* ones but nowadays *synthetic* or artificial colours are often used. In Great Britain only a small number of synthetic colours can be added to food—these are colours that are believed to be harmless. The use of any other synthetic colours is illegal.

The addition of colour to food can make it much more attractive. For example, strawberries that have been preserved using sodium metabisulphite lose all their colour and are nearly white. Such strawberries are used in making jam and as white strawberry jam would be very unpopular a red dye is used to restore the strawberry colour. When peas are prepared for canning the bright green colour of fresh peas is turned into a dull olive green. The original colour is restored by the addition of a synthetic green colour. Margarine would be an unattractive off-white colour unless colour was added, and so a synthetic yellow colour is added to make its appearance resemble that of butter.

FLAVOUR

When you have a bad cold your sense of flavour is very poor and you cannot smell the aroma of roasting coffee nor recognize the taste of chicken. Your sense of flavour comes partly from your nose which enables you to *smell* the aroma of food and partly from your mouth which enables you to *taste* food.

Our appreciation of smell is part of the enjoyment of food and the smell of an appetizing meal stimulates the flow of our digestive juices and so aids our powers of digestion. The smell or aroma of food is due to substances which vaporize, i.e. turn into gas when exposed to air; such substances are said to be *volatile*. When coffee beans are ground and roasted and when coffee is being made a splendid aroma is produced. This is because volatile flavouring substances present in the coffee are vaporized and we smell the vapour. If coffee is percolated or brewed for a considerable time the resulting coffee drink has lost most of its flavour.

★★★ **Keypoint.** When preparing coffee or cooking food which contains volatile flavours, great care must be taken to heat the food gently and for the shortest possible time so that loss of flavour is kept to a minimum. When there is a delicious aroma in the kitchen just remember that this means less flavour in the food!

When volatile flavours are added to food, e.g. oil of lemon, rum or vanilla, great care should then be taken to prevent them from being lost by over-heating.

★ ? Where wine is used to improve the flavour of a cooked food, should the wine be added at the beginning of the cooking process or is it better to add it near the end? (The alcohol in wine is very volatile.)

Taste

★★★ **Keypoint.** The taste of food is detected by taste buds on the tongue which is able to detect four distinct tastes:

Salt – Sour – Bitter – Sweet

Some foods have just one taste—e.g. sugar which is sweet—but others have more than one taste. For example, bitter lemon is sweet and bitter at the same time and sweet pickle is sweet and sour at the same time. The taste of food is so important that in factories where food is made on a large scale people are employed to taste the food and make sure it is up to standard (see photo).

Saltiness. Boiled potatoes and cabbage cooked without any salt in the cooking water have a very unattractive taste, and even when they have been salted during cooking many people like to add more salt before they eat them. Salt is able to bring out the flavour of food and make it much more attractive. Even porridge which is normally eaten with sugar tastes much better if salt is added as well.

Salt is not only used to improve flavour but it is a nutrient as we saw in Chapter 6, and the mineral elements which it contains—do you remember what they are?—are needed by the body. How-

231

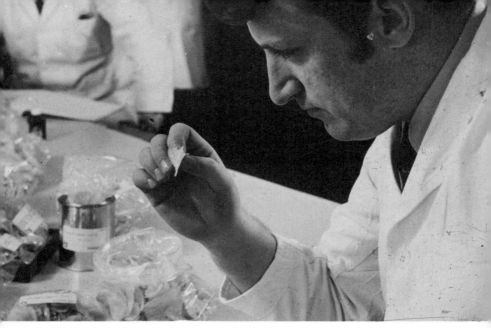

Taste-testing is an important job when foods are made on a large scale. Here the seasonings used in crisps are being checked

ever, even if we don't add salt during cooking, food contains enough salt for normal needs.

Sourness. We are all familiar with sour foods such as vinegar, salad cream and most fruit. The taste of sourness is due to the presence of *acids* in the food. Citrus fruits, for example, are sour because they contain *citric acid*. Citric acid itself is often used as a flavouring agent and it is the basis of lemon drinks in powder form. The sharpness in the taste of grapes is due to the presence of *tartaric acid*, and this acid is added to fruit drinks and to boiled sweets to give them a slightly sharp taste and it is also one of the ingredients of baking powder (more usually a *salt* of tartaric acid is used).

Acids are often used not just to impart flavour but also to preserve food. The best known example of this is the use of vinegar to preserve vegetables such as onions.

In some foods a sour taste is an indication that it has gone 'bad' due to the production of acid substances in the food. For example, milk on storage becomes sour as the milk sugar, called *lactose*, is converted into *lactic acid*. Thus whereas fresh milk is slightly sweet, milk that has been stored for too long is sour.

232

★★★ Keypoint.

Lactose   → *storage*   Lactic acid

(fresh milk)   (sour milk)

This is another example of a change brought about by enzymes.

Although souring of milk is usually thought of as being undesirable it is made use of in the preparation of fermented milks like yoghourt, and in the production of butter and cheese.

Bitterness. An ordinary orange is sour but not bitter whereas Seville oranges have a bitter taste. Although a Seville orange has a much less pleasant taste than an ordinary orange its quality of bitterness is valuable in making marmalade. In marmalade the bitterness and sourness of the Seville oranges is balanced by the large amount of sugar used. If marmalade is made from ordinary oranges it has a sickly sweet taste which many people dislike.

★ ? The pips of Seville oranges contain bitter substances. Why do you think it is that in making marmalade the pips are boiled along with the fruit?

The bitterness of coffee is one of its attractive qualities and it is due to the presence of *caffeine.* Caffeine is also responsible for the bitterness of tea, as well as its mild stimulating action. If tea is allowed to 'brew' for too long it becomes unpleasantly bitter because too much caffeine infuses into it.

The universal popularity of *Coca Cola* is due to the careful balancing of sweetness (from sugar) with sourness (from acid) and bitterness (from quinine).

Sweetness. The sweetness of various sugars was discussed on page 17. The attractiveness of many foods is due to their sweet taste, and this is particularly true of many modern convenience foods.

★★ **Activity.** Note down on a piece of paper twenty convenience foods that are attractive because they are sweet. (You may like to time yourself and compare your time with that of other members of your class.)

Apart from natural sweeteners one artificial sweetener is used in food and that is *saccharin*. Saccharin is about 300 times as sweet as sugar and so very little of it is needed to make food acceptably sweet. Unfortunately it is not a perfect sweetening agent because, unlike sugar, it is also bitter and it leaves an unpleasant bitter taste in the mouth after the taste of sweetness has gone. On the other hand because saccharin has no energy value it is used by slimmers as a substitute for sugar. Artificial sweeteners are of great value to diabetics who are unable to digest sugar.

Natural flavours

We have already noted that the flavour of food is important to its enjoyment and so it is not surprising that flavours are added to food to increase its acceptability. Rice and potatoes are two examples of food that would be very dull if they were boiled and served alone without the addition of any flavour. The use of salt in cooking and the addition of salt, pepper, mustard and sauces to food after cooking all help to improve the palatability of food.

Different methods of cooking produce different flavours in food and it is important to remember this when deciding how to cook a particular food. The flavour of strawberries, for example, is due to the presence of over 150 different substances, many of which are volatile. This means that strawberries are best eaten raw because on cooking volatile flavours are lost and the flavour deteriorates.

★ ? In making strawberry jam it is usually recommended that the strawberries should be boiled as quickly as possible for the minimum time. Why is this?

If food is cooked by roasting this produces quite a different flavour from that produced by boiling. For example, roast potatoes taste quite different from boiled potatoes. This is mainly because at the high temperatures used in roasting new flavouring substances and a brown colour are produced. Similar changes take place in the toasting of bread, the frying of chips and in coffee roasting. The attractive golden-brown colour and good flavour of cornflakes and crisps are also due to similar changes that take place during cooking.

Herbs and spices are used in cooking to improve the flavour of food. *Herbs* are plants with soft stems and the whole of the green plant is used for flavouring. Perhaps you will be most familiar with garden *mint* which is used to flavour peas and new potatoes. You will also know *parsley* which is sometimes used as a garnish to make food (e.g. fish) look more attractive. It is also used chopped to flavour foods such as potatoes and as a sauce with fish. *Thyme* and *sage* are also herbs and they are commonly used in stuffing.

Spices not only add their own flavour to food but are able to bring out the natural flavour of the food itself. Spices are usually taken from one part of the plant. For example, *cinnamon* is part of the bark of the plant, *pepper* is a fruit and *mustard* is a seed. These spices are usually used ground up as a fine powder.

Spices are also used to improve the colour and appearance of food. For example, *paprika* has an attractive red colour and is

Many different herbs and spices are used to flavour food. The photograph shows a selection including the well-known herbs *sage* and *rosemary* in the jars. Spices come from many different parts of a plant; you can probably identify seeds, barks and fruits

235

sometimes added as a powder (e.g. to stuffed eggs) and sometimes added to a sauce (e.g. to tomato sauce used for baked beans).

★ ? Do you think that herbs such as garden mint have a better flavour when fresh or when dried? Can you give a reason?

Flavour enhancers. Substances which have little or no flavour themselves but which can bring out or enhance the natural flavour of foods are known as *flavour enhancers*. The most widely used flavour enhancer is the salt of an amino acid and is known as *monosodium glutamate*, MSG. Even when added in small amounts—about 0.1%—it brings out the natural flavour of meat, fish and vegetable foods.

MSG is now added to many convenience foods such as canned fish and meat products and canned soups such as mushroom and chicken. It is also used to enhance the flavour of dehydrated vegetables and many soup powders. In the home the powdered salt can be sprinkled onto food before cooking or afterwards.

Substances known as *ribonucleotides* are also used as flavour enhancers. They occur naturally in animal tissues and yeast extracts and contribute to their meaty taste. They are used to enhance the flavour of many meat and fish products.

This meal does not only look attractive but it has been well chosen to provide an interesting variety of different textures. Try to describe the textures of the foods you can see

TEXTURE

★★ **Activity.** Eat samples of the following: apple, cream, bread. Try to describe what they *feel* like in the mouth.

The feel of food in the mouth is an important part of our appreciation of it, and yet you probably found it quite difficult to describe the feel of the food in the activity above. This is because there are so many different factors involved in the feel or *texture* of food.

For example, one of the most important is *consistency*.

★★★ **Keypoint.** Consistency can be described in many different ways, some of which are as follows:

> Creamy – Smooth – Tender – Tough – Brittle – Chewy
> Gritty – Slimy – Flaky – Crisp – Watery – Thick

★ **?** For each of the words above can you think of one food as an example? For example, crisp—cornflakes.

In terms of texture there are two main types of food:

1. Those containing the basic structure of the plant or animal from which food comes; e.g. potatoes and cabbage, meat and fish.
2. Those that have lost their plant or animal structure, e.g. bread and biscuits, ice-cream and instant whip, sausages, jam and meat paste.

★★★ **Keypoint.** Many convenience foods require very little chewing because during processing the cellular structure of the plant or animal material is broken down to give a product with a smooth texture. These foods are often popular with young people, but eating too many of such foods can be boring. Biting and chewing food is part of the enjoyment of eating as well as being good for the teeth.

Smooth jelly-like foods usually contain either *starch*, *gelatin* or *pectin*. These substances are able to absorb water to form a jelly-like structure called a *gel*. For example, gelatin will form a solid gel even though it contains 99% water! (see table).

237

Contrasting textures. **Part of the attraction of this lemon meringue pie is the contrast in texture between the light foamy meringue topping and the smooth jelly-like lemon filling. The tender but crisp texture of the pastry provides another contrast**

SUBSTANCES THAT FORM SMOOTH JELLY-LIKE FOODS

Substance	Examples
Starch	Instant puddings, custards, blancmanges pie-fillings, glazes for fruit flans
Gelatin	Jellies, mousse, ice-cream, cream desserts (e.g. Bavarian creams), aspic jelly and glazes for meat pies
Pectin	Jam, marmalade

Creamy textures can be produced by dispersing oil through water in the form of very tiny droplets which are so small that they can only be seen through a microscope. Salad cream and mayonnaise, and milk and cream are familiar examples. They are known as *emulsions.*

13 Diet, health and disease

You will remember that a *balanced diet* (page 125) is one that supplies us with all the essential nutrients in the correct proportions to our needs. To-day most people in Britain receive in their diet all required nutrients whereas a century ago this was not so. At the beginning of this century, for instance, poorer folk lived almost entirely on bread and tea and general health was relatively poor; rickets (page 109) and malnutrition were commonplace.

To-day we are much healthier and our standard of living is much higher than a century ago. Clean water, efficient disposal of sewage, advances in medicine, better housing as well as a healthier diet have all contributed to this. A hundred years ago *infectious diseases* such as cholera, tuberculosis, typhoid, smallpox and scarlet fever were common whereas to-day in Britain they are almost unknown. Modern medicine has enabled us to eliminate these diseases which used to be the main cause of death.

Nowadays it is generally accepted that our diet is important in keeping us healthy. It is also accepted that if certain nutrients, such as vitamins, are lacking from our diet we may suffer from a deficiency disease (page 100). The discovery of vitamins and their role in keeping us fit did not become clear until the beginning of this century. It showed that diet is a major factor in causing disease as well as in keeping us healthy.

★ ? What deficiency disease can you name? What causes them?

New diseases of the Western world

★★★ **Keypoint.** In Britain to-day people do not die from infectious diseases. One in three die from coronary heart disease (CHD), one in four from cancer and one in seven from strokes.

These 'new' diseases, which are not infectious, seem to creep up on people unawares and only become apparent in middle age or old age. These diseases are almost unknown in Third World (undeveloped) countries where people live in simple village communities. The new diseases do not have any single cause— several different factors are involved, and one of these is diet. In general it seems that it is our Western way of life that is responsible for them.

★★★ **Keypoint.** Statements in newspapers and on TV often say that a particular food is 'bad' for you and causes disease. It is very rare for a food to be bad for you—unless you eat too much of it—and it is also very rare for any one food to be the cause of a disease.

An example will illustrate this *keypoint*. Sugar is often quoted as being bad for you but it is more accurate to say that *too much sugar* is bad for you. Sugar has been blamed for many ills, particularly for obesity, tooth decay, coronary heart disease (CHD) and diabetes. Sugar is certainly bad for teeth and bad for slimming but we cannot say that sugar *causes* a disease although it does contribute to several, particularly obesity and tooth decay.

Fats. Many people believe that we eat more fat than is good for us. There is some evidence, but no proof, that links the fat in our diet with CHD and other diseases. *Saturated fats* (page 26)—but not *polyunsaturated fats*—are the ones under suspicion and so it seems sensible to limit the amount of saturated fat that we eat.

The most important sources of saturated fats in the diet are (in order) meat, butter and milk while the most important sources of polyunsaturated fats are soft margarines and some oils.

SOURCES OF SATURATED AND POLYUNSATURATED FATS

High in saturated fats	Dairy products	Butter, cream, milk, lard, cheese
	Meat	Liver, lamb, beef, pork
	Others	Coconut oil, palm kernel oil, hard margarine
High in polyunsaturated fats	Vegetable oils	Corn (maize) oil, soya bean oil, sunflower oil, sunflower seed oil
	Nuts	Most, except coconut and cashew nuts
	Margarines	Many soft varieties especially soya and sunflower

The table above shows which foods you need to limit if you want to eat less saturated fats and what you should select if you want to increase your intake of polyunsaturated fat.

Salt. Salt is essential to our health (page 3) but most people obtain much more than they need from their food; in Britain we eat on average about three times as much as we need. At first sight this does not seem to be important because any excess salt is removed by the kidneys and passes out of the body in the urine. However, as salt intake increases so does blood pressure—and high blood pressure is thought to be a major risk factor in CHD. It is possible, therefore, that too much salt is harmful.

★★★ **Keypoint.** We obtain the salt in our diet in four ways:
1. In fresh food.
2. Added by manufacturers to processed food.
3. Added in cooking.
4. Added as table salt.

We obtain all the salt we need from fresh food—meat, milk, fish and eggs for example. It is wise therefore not to eat too many processed foods high in salt, and not to add too much salt in cooking or at table. Limiting salt intake can do no harm and may contribute to good health, especially for those with a tendency to high blood pressure.

★★ **Activity.** Very young infants cannot tolerate too much salt and baby foods should therefore contain no added salt. Check the baby foods on sale at your local supermarket and see if any contain added salt.

Foods which are high in salt include bacon, sausages and most meat products (but not fresh meat), kippers, cheese and salted butter. Yeast extract has the highest salt content of any food.

Dietary fibre. ★★★ **Keypoint.** We have already seen that:
1. Dietary fibre consists of that part of plant foods which cannot be digested by the body.

A selection of wholefoods. How many can you identify? Do they all contain fibre?

2. It is largely a mixture of polysaccharides.
3. It provides the body with bulk and this is important because it makes the contents of the bowels soft and bulky and so prevents constipation.

During the last hundred years many people have moved from villages into towns and at the same time the total population has increased. This means that more food is needed and that the need to store, transport and preserve food has increased. Food can be preserved in a number of ways and it often involves adding something to the food e.g. a preservative or removing something e.g. water. The latter often involves removing much of the original plant material which is rich in fibre; this is known as *refining*. White sugar is a perfect example of a refined food; it is almost one hundred per cent sucrose—all the fibre and water of the original sugar cane or sugar beet has been removed. White bread is another example. During the milling or refining process 30 per cent of the original wheat grain is removed and the white flour produced contains only one third of the fibre present in the whole grain.

Over the past century our consumption of fibre-rich foods has gradually decreased as consumption of bread and potatoes has fallen and consumption of refined convenience foods has increased. It is estimated that our intake of fibre has halved since the middle of the last century. Although our intake of fibre from fruit and vegetables has increased over this period, this has been more than offset by the reduced amount of cereal fibre that we eat.

Some people believe that many of the new non-infectious diseases that are common in the Western world are partly due to lack of fibre in our modern diet. They point out that in undeveloped countries where fibre intake is high these disease are almost unknown. Diseases linked with low fibre intake include constipation, diverticular disease, cancer of the colon and diabetes.

It is generally agreed that a low-fibre diet is a cause of constipation and of diverticular disease, and the treatment for the latter has been changed accordingly. Until recently it was treated by giving a *low-fibre* diet whereas to-day it is treated with a *high-fibre* diet! It is also believed that a high-fibre diet reduces the risk of cancer of the colon.

The table below shows some foods which are high or fairly high in fibre. Where an average portion of a food contains six or more grams of fibre the food is given as high in fibre; where it contains 3–6 g fibre it is given as medium in fibre.

243

FOODS RICH IN FIBRE

High in fibre (per portion)	Baked beans, sweetcorn, wholemeal bread, All-bran, peas, stewed prunes and apricots, blackberries and raspberries
Medium in fibre (per portion)	Wheat bran, bran flakes, brown bread, muesli, Weetabix, baked potato (eaten with skin), Spring greens, runner beans, carrots, baked and stewed apple, bananas

★★★ **Keypoint.** A snack of baked beans in tomato sauce on a slice of wholemeal toast is the 'Best buy' for fibre. It is also 'Best value for money' for a simple meal that is rich in fibre, high in food value and cheap—an unbeatable combination!

How much fibre should we eat? People living in undeveloped countries and who do not suffer from our new diseases eat at least 40 g fibre each day—that is twice as much as we eat in Britain—and this seems a reasonable target to aim for. We could achieve this quite simply by including the following in a day's meals: All-bran or bran flakes for breakfast, a baked potato and peas for lunch and baked beans on wholemeal toast for tea.

★ ? Can you plan a day's meals that contain at least one fibre-rich food in each meal? Can you name three foods that contain no fibre?

Goals for a healthy diet

A healthy diet will be a balanced one; it will also be an attractive one (page 135). A healthy diet is also one which provides us with enough food for our bodies' needs—but not too much. In the West one major factor contributing to ill-health is obesity, so eating less—especially of energy-rich foods—is desirable for many people.

★★★ **Keypoint.** Two helpful slogans for a healthy diet are *'Moderation in all things'* and *'Variety is best'*. Moderation in all things means that we don't eat too much of any one food and Variety is best means that we eat a wide variety of different foods.

Diet in Western countries often includes many fatty foods, foods rich in sugar and refined convenience foods. Some people also eat considerable amounts of salt and drink large amounts of alcohol. Such diets may not be healthy and may contribute to the increase in the new diseases. In recent years a number of countries have produced sets of dietary goals for health. The following set of simple guidelines is based on these dietary goals and provides a sound basis for improving diet and health in Western countries:

1. Avoid being overweight by eating less energy-rich foods.
2. Avoid eating too much fat, especially saturated fat.
3. Avoid too much sugar and sugar-rich foods.
4. Avoid too much salt.
5. Avoid too much alcohol.
6. Eat enough bread (preferably wholemeal), fruit and vegetables. These provide fibre and can with advantage replace sugar-rich foods, fatty foods and highly refined convenience foods.

One thing is certain: if you follow the guidelines given above you cannot possibly do any harm—they are designed to improve health.

★★★ **Keypoint.** A healthy lifestyle including some exercise and avoiding smoking will also contribute to health.

METRIC AND IMPERIAL UNITS

The following table shows how non-metric units may be converted into metric equivalents.

	Non-metric	Metric equivalent
Energy	1 kilocalorie (Cal)	4200 joules (J) 4·2 kilojoules (kJ)
Temperature	32° Fahrenheit (F) 212° Fahrenheit (F) To convert °F into °C: −32° and then ×5/9	0° Celsius (C) 100° Celsius (C)
Volume	1·8 pints 1 pint 1 gallon	1 litre (l) 1000 millilitres (ml) 568 millilitres (ml) 4·5 litres (l)
Weight	1 ounce (oz) 1 pound (lb) 2·2 pounds (lb)	28·4 grammes (g) 454 grammes (g) 1 kilogramme (kg)
Length	1 inch (in.) 1 foot (ft) 39·4 inches (in.)	2·5 centimetres (cm) 30·5 centimetres (cm) 100 centimetres (cm) 1 metre (m)

PRACTICAL WORKING EQUIVALENTS

The following equivalents, though not accurate, have been agreed for practical working purposes:

	Non-metric	Metric equivalent
Volume	1 pint	500 millilitres
Weight	1 ounce	25 grammes

Index

Honey, 14, 17
Hydrogen, 8
Hydrogenation, 50
Hydrolysis, 16, 31
Hygiene, 170
    and waste, 185
    in the kitchen, 175, 185
    personal, 173, 186

Infectious diseases, 239
Instant pudding, 167
Intestinal juice, 40
Inversion, 17
Invert-sugar, 17
Iodine, 29, 112
Iron, 29, 111

Jam, 17, 20, 157
Joule, 43
Junket, 77

Kilojoule, 43

Lactose, 16, 34, 78
Life, 1
Lignin, 19, 222
Liver, 129
Lunch, 13, 133, 134, 184

Maize, 63
Maltose, 16
Margarine, 50, 71
Meals, 128
    for adults, 141
    for invalids, 142
    for school-children, 141
    for slimming, 148
    for the elderly, 143
    for the very young, 139
    for vegetarians, 144
    packed, 145

value for money, 137
    well balanced, 132
Meal planning, 125, 129
    general principles of, 131, 135
Meat, 89, 138
    chilled, 164
    cooking of, 197, 217
    tenderness of, 89, 218
Meringues, 24, 203
Micro-organisms, 152
    and new food sources, 97
Milk, 50, 76, 209
    as a body-builder, 77
    curdling of, 78, 205
    dried, 82
    evaporated, 82
    homogenized, 80
    pasteurized, 80
    sterilised, 80
    sweetened condensed, 82
    treatment of, 80
Milling, 55
Mineral elements, 7, 28, 75, 81, 110, 124
    effects of cooking on, 198
    for body-building, 75
Molasses, 69
Molecule, 9
Monosaccharide, 14
Monosodium glutamate, 236
Moulds, 152
Myosin, 90

Nitrogen, 11, 21
Nutrients, 5
    nature of, 13
    recommended amount of, 126
Nutrition, 6
Nutritive value of,

250